JOURNEY WITH THE WORLD'S BEST TRAVEL WRITERS

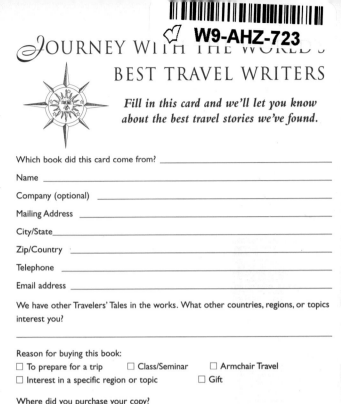

W9-AHZ-723

Fill in this card and we'll let you know about the best travel stories we've found.

Which book did this card come from? _____

Name _____

Company (optional) _____

Mailing Address _____

City/State _____

Zip/Country _____

Telephone _____

Email address _____

We have other Travelers' Tales in the works. What other countries, regions, or topics interest you?

_____

Reason for buying this book:
☐ To prepare for a trip   ☐ Class/Seminar   ☐ Armchair Travel
☐ Interest in a specific region or topic   ☐ Gift

Where did you purchase your copy?
☐ Bookstore   ☐ Direct from O'Reilly   ☐ Received as gift   ☐ Online   ☐ Other

☐   Please send me the Travelers' Tales Catalog
☐   I do not want my name given to outside mailing lists

Give us three names and addresses of people you think would like Travelers' Tales and we will enter your name in our monthly drawing to receive one free Travelers' Tales book of your choice!

Name _____
Address _____
City/State/Zip _____

Name _____
Address _____
City/State/Zip _____

Name _____
Address _____
City/State/Zip _____

Gutsy MAMAS

TRAVEL
TIPS
and
WISDOM
for
MOTHERS
on the
ROAD

Gutsy MAMAS

TRAVEL
TIPS
and
WISDOM
for
MOTHERS
on the
ROAD

BY MARYBETH BOND

Travelers' Tales, Inc.
San Francisco, California

Distributed by
O'Reilly and Associates
101 Morris Street, Sebastopol, CA 95472

Gutsy Mamas: Travel Tips and Wisdom for Mothers on the Road
By Marybeth Bond

Cover design by Kathryn Heflin
Interior design by Susan Bailey
Cover photographs:
- © Marybeth Bond and daughter canoeing in northern Canada
- © Victor Englebert, Niger. Sahara. Tuareq mother of three moving camp. Husband away with camel herd.
- © Marybeth Bond and mother, Grand Canyon
- © Rick Ridgeway/Adventure Photo & Film. Mother and daughter getting water, Telluride, Colorado
- Peter Arnold, Inc. © M. Laboureur. Woman carrying baby in wash basin on head, Central African Republic.

Printing History
November 1997:   First Edition

ISBN: 1-885-211-20-1

TABLE OF CONTENTS

$\mathcal{I}$ NTRODUCTION

It is a wise parent who gives his children roots and wings.
—*Chinese Proverb*

———

IT HAS ALWAYS TAKEN courage, stamina, and self-sacrifice to be a mother, and this is especially true in our hectic modern world. Indeed, bearing a child and giving birth are the very definition of gutsy. As a woman, it also takes guts to travel boldly, to leave the world of home and job and venture into the uncertainty of the open road. Historically, a mother's sphere has been "inside" the private realm of the home, where she is both nurturing and dependent. Today, as more women are working "outside" the home, achieving new levels of independence, a mother's world has expanded and is filled with new opportunities, many which include travel.

We all admire those women who climb forbidding Himalayan peaks, kayak Class V rivers in far-off jungles, or those female executives who speak the argot of international finance whether they are in Paris or Kuala Lumpur. We also shake our heads in wonder at the strength of immigrant mothers of yore, and those tenacious women around the world who are refugees today, nurturing families under appalling conditions. There is no shortage of Gutsy Mamas on this planet, and there never has been.

But the rest of us, who lead quieter, more ordinary lives, nonetheless want to share the gift of travel with our children, our spouses, our grandchildren, our aging parents, in whatever way we can. We may be women who traveled once as students, women who may have satisfied the early tuggings of wanderlust, but who now have children and spouses. We may be women who have not traveled at

7

all but who want to make our dreams real. We may be women who not only raise (or have raised) the children, but take care of the home and pay the bills, doing the dance of the mundane. The purpose of this book is to inspire, encourage, and celebrate all mothers.

Like my previous books, *A Woman's World* and *Gutsy Women*, this book is not just about travel, it is about taking risks, learning to be bold, confident—in a word, gutsy. *Gutsy Mamas* contains more than tips on how to travel as a woman and mother, it is about redefining ourselves in the world as voyagers who not only nurture our families but enrich those who come into contact with us whenever and wherever we travel. It is also about how to let each trip enrich us so that we come back to our daily lives renewed, with a fresh perspective on ourselves as mothers and individuals.

Unfortunately, mothering is too often devalued. But if we take a good look at our own mothers and ourselves, we'll recognize just how courageous we already are. The anecdotes in *Gutsy Mamas* will renew your respect for the many mothers who are drawn to explore the cities, mountains, trails, and rivers of the world in greater and greater numbers, and who are taking their families with them. We are teaching our children, by example, that when we walk out into the world, not only do we learn and grow from our travel experiences, we have something more to share with others.

Women are flexing their economic muscle and the travel industry is reflecting this trend. Over 70% of all travel decisions of all types are made by women. Over 63% of all overseas travelers on adventure trips are female. Increasingly, moms are traveling without their children or partner. And mothers recently divorced or widowed are no longer staying at home. Mothers are taking to the roads, rails, trails, and skies with different companions—their own mothers, sisters, and friends.

Why do we travel? We look for more than rest, relaxation, and fun. For most women, travel satisfies deep emotional and psychological needs. Many of us have learned to go into the woods when we feel out of balance. When we return to nature we are soothed and nurtured by the earth. Testing ourselves in the outdoors allows us to break through limiting concepts of ourselves, overcome fears, to become empowered and rejuvenated. Similarly, travel helps us reclaim our sense of self and strength. We can break with tradition, try on new roles, cross boundaries imposed by society.

In our increasingly hectic, time-compressed lives, we are more and more separated from each other and from a sense of community. Staying home with young children, for instance, can lead to isolation, and a demanding career has its own ways of interrupting family life. An entrepreneur, often working out of a home office, has little time for camaraderie. The increased role of technology has had a detrimental impact on many women's lives, leading to less personal contact with other women. We often don't have time to see friends and many of us no longer communicate through written letters or phone calls, sending brief email messages instead.

How do we reconnect? How do we find camaraderie and support? Where do we find the strength in sisterhood which past generations took for granted? One way is through travel. The rewards of travel are different for women than they are for men, simply because women travel differently than men. How so? We connect more! Where women go, relationships follow. We pause more to listen and move in and out of the lives of those we meet on the way, from encounters with other mothers and children, to special friendships.

None of us are "gutsy" all the time. Prior to most of my big trips, I have doubts. I get the jitters, I second-guess myself. I need words of encouragement to boost my confidence. In this book you'll encounter words of wisdom from intrepid traveling moms. These women, of all ages, are my mentors, my role models. Their words help to break the inertia that settles in me from time to time, and they remind me of the rewards of getting out there under a different sky.

How do you begin? And if you are a veteran traveler, how do you begin again? *Gutsy Mamas* will give you the encouragement and practical advice to get you on the road. Do not let time or money be an obstacle—where there is a Gutsy Mama there is a way. Follow some of the creative tips in the text and refamiliarize yourself with the many things that you already know. At the back of the book are resources that will help answer specific questions such as where to find information on family dude ranches in the West, barge trips in France, safaris in Africa, mother-daughter adventures, women-only tours, or volunteer opportunities overseas.

If you are a man reading this book, consider giving it wrapped up with an airplane ticket to a mother you love.

There is no greater gift than that of sharing wisdom and love. We must tell our tales of exploration and discovery, of our human needs, our desires, our failures and our triumphs. And thus we will pass down, from mother to daughter and son, from grandmother to grandchild, the courage, patience and selflessness inherent in Motherhood. And we will share, through our stories, the strength to step out the door and live our dreams.

I

JOYS AND BENEFITS OF TRAVEL WITH CHILDREN

Once you have traveled, the voyage never ends, but it is played
out over and over again in the quietest chambers…the mind
can never break off from the journe

Pat Conroy, American w

IRONICALLY, IT IS WHEN we ar
most easily drift away from the de
we treasure. By that I mean
our lives become so domi-
nated by routines, job
stresses, and the different
demands of each child at
each stage, that we can easily lose perspective on what
is most important to us.

When traveling, my hus-
band and children and I
converge back into the core
of this magical relationship
that is family. We depend on
each other for guidance,
help, and fun. We deal with
unforseen problems and ac-
cidental delights, and get to

*Fo
my so
in Italy for a
me by saying "that was the best
thing you ever did, Mom." I
was touched. He feels it had a
tremendous impact on his life
because it exposed him to a different culture and taught him
at an early age that the world
was not all like Iowa.*

◆

*Barbara Gash, 70, retired flight
attendant, volunteer English
teacher in Warsaw*

know each other better. We weave a tapestry of common stories to tell over and over. And when we return home from
our travels, all is new, and we are closer and more connected.

11

Time on the road lends itself to long talks, story-telling, games, and reading aloud. Parents whose lives are harried at home get to spend a different kind of time with their children. A family vacation is a time out from day-to-day life when every person has a chance to be heard, to listen, and to participate. A family pulls together to become a self-sufficient team—deciphering maps, interpreting road signs, working through problems, and making decisions. Children have open-ended play time and interaction. They become better friends as they rely upon each other, even as they squabble more and learn to resolve disputes in a different way than they might at home.

Children learn by actively participating in the greater world around them.

All three of our children have spent two weeks during high school summers in Tijuana, Mexico. These have been life-changing trips, where they've grown in compassion, gratitude, and benevolence. Our son, Tim, 15, recently demonstrated one of the lessons he'd learned. As we were returning to our car after a Mariner's game in Seattle, we passed a beggar. Tim asked me for the bag of cookies I had in my purse and ran back to where the man was sitting, just to share what he had with someone who had less. As an adult, I know that at times there are reasons other than genuine need which causes people to beg, and I will teach him wisdom to go along with his heart—but no amount of counsel could ever give him the kind and generous heart that comes out of compassion.

◆

Joyce Williams, 40+, author of
The Lady Rose

When they visit non-English speaking countries, they get to experience what it feels like to be an outsider, a "foreigner." They return home and look at foreigners in their own country with more understanding. Exposure to different cultures and people teaches children tolerance and compassion.

And they also learn how to handle difficulties on the road. It is normal to experience delays, for things to go wrong, and to get tired and cranky. Taking cues from you, they can learn patience, how to laugh in the face of adversity and keep going. *Travel is one of your child's best teachers.*

The rewards of traveling with children are immense for parents too—the opportunity to enhance your own capacity for spontaneity, patience, and empathy, as well as to know yourself in a more profound way.

When asked to recall the most vivid memories of childhood, most adults recount brief moments in time when they were actively engaged or deeply touched. One of these intense moments for my daughter was when she looked a whale in the eye and the whale looked back, as we floated in a wooden skiff in a lagoon in Baja, Mexico.

In these warm waters, female whales birth and nurse. The connection between the mother whales, their babies, and us made a deep impression on my daughter and intensified her passion for marine biology. Her involvement with the whales not only will live longer in her memory than what she learns from reading or seeing a documentary, it brought her school learning to vivid life.

We also traveled the desert backroads of Baja exploring

> *My daughters' relationships with each other changed when we traveled for five months in Europe. Before the trip, the oldest would drop her sisters when her friends came to play. Traveling together, they became best friends as well as sisters with favorite memories to rehash—singing songs from a balcony in Annecy, France on New Year's Eve, making butter on a farm in the Charente Maritime, grimacing and laughing over the terrible cafeteria food in their school in the Alps, made by the janitor.*
>
> ◆
>
> *Wenda Brewster, Ph.D., 49, writer*

the real Mexico, away from resorts. My children were surprised to see people living in shacks, villages with unpaved streets. They observed kids their own age, dressed in uniforms, coming home from school, linked arm-in-arm, laughing, children playing in cement playgrounds devoid of fancy swings or slides. They learned about the bigger world as they compared it with their own and they saw that there are different ways of living, different ways to be happy.

Traveling with your children is one of the best investments you can make in the future of your family. Everyone benefits: deepening the commitment of each member to the family, strengthening sibling relationships, savoring moments of expressed love, and creating memories that last a lifetime.

_____ ⚜ _____

Children can experience the world without leaving home. Starting with my 3- year-old and continuing for 12 years, my family hosted foreign visitors via the Foreign Student Service Council in Washington, D.C. Our guests included a 17-year-old student from Denmark, a 58-year-old retired opera singer from Norway, a Swedish Naval officer, an African tribesman who would one day be chief of his village. These were people from all stations of life who shared with us as we shared with them. After 25 years, I can still close my eyes and revel in the aria sung by the Norwegian opera singer. The cost of this travel was nominal: a place to sleep and a few meals provided us with travel experiences that were unique and personalized.

◆

Diana Culbertson, Ph.D., 61, retired teacher and librarian

TIPS

➤ Involve children in the planning, preparation, and the calendar countdown. The excitement of anticipation is half the fun of travel.

➢ History "sticks" when
children actually see
where it took place. It
makes a far stronger
impression than most
books alone can. Back-
ground material will
enhance the experi-
ence, however, so
check out relevant
books from the library
before you go.

➢ Learn some elements of
a second language as a
family before you travel
to a foreign country.
Your children will not
only benefit from be-
ginning to learn a new
language, they will get
to use it practically and
make friends more
easily.

_My parents had lived in Texas
and Louisiana all their lives
when, in their 30s, my father
was transferred to Kuwait.
Camel caravans on the trade
routes to Mecca and Baghdad
passed our doorway with veiled
women in wood carriers. We
also visited the pyramids in
Egypt, Basra, the birthplace of
civilization, and saw the great
capitals of Europe on the way
home. They told us this would
be the only chance we'd have in
our lives to see the world, but
for my brother and me, it
opened up the whole world,
and both of us have become
lifelong lovers of travel to far-
away places._

◆

_Lynn Ferrin, 50+,
Editor of Via Magazine_

➢ Trips are a great way to make geography come alive.
Show your children the intended route on the map,
and explain how long it will take to go from point A
to point B. Get a felt pen and draw your route; it will
be a wonderful souvenir and memory prompt later.

➢ Explore the differences between a standard Mercator
projection map and a map such as the Peters
Projection, which shows countries in their proper
geographic scale.

➤ Travel teaches children how to be flexible, as the family encounters delays, cancellations, reservation mix-ups, closed attractions, full restaurants, rude people. They will learn to remain calm and enjoy the adventure if *you* do.

➤ When you select books to take on a trip, include juvenile books you can read aloud to your children as well as adult books such as the abridged version of *Moby Dick*. The Narnia Series by C. S. Lewis is ideal because the stories, morals, and vocabulary appeal to both child and adult.

➤ Children learn responsibility when they compose their own packing lists and pack their own bags. It builds confidence and decision-making. Show them your lists and discuss how you are packing and making plans in advance. They can make sure that their favorite clothes are clean the day before departure. It is a good idea to confirm that they have the essentials.

➤ Memories are made from brief moments. A trip that lasts a few days or weeks in reality will last a lifetime. Children will never forget bathing under a water-

As a child I only went back and forth to grandma's house, a four-hour drive from home. So today I am passionate about traveling. As soon as I graduated from college, I went abroad to live and have been nurturing all those fantasies I had as a child ever since. Now, as a mom, I give my son the opportunities to explore the world in a way I never did—he's held baby orangutans in Borneo and snorkeled in Thailand. We're making up for lost time.

◆

Marilyn Staff, 40+, tour company founder

fall, eating mangos on the beach under a full moon, walking across an airport tarmac, or mimicking unforgettable characters encountered on the road.

➤ Write in a travel journal describing funny situations, conversations, even disasters.

➤ Stop at tourist information booths or offices. Your children can pick up brochures and create scrapbooks from them. You may also learn about a festival or a museum—or a cave—

> *My father encouraged us to travel early in our lives. My introduction was horse pack trips into the Sierra Nevada mountains at the age of 3. He always wanted to travel NOW because he didn't want to see the world from a wheelchair. He died of a massive coronary at age 47, but he had seen the world. He and my mom had traveled to Europe twice and they weren't at all wealthy. His philosophy stuck with me and got me on the road.*
>
> ◆
>
> *Linda Liscom, 60, Board of Directors, Great Old Broads for Wilderness*

you were unaware of and may discover a family member has an interest you never suspected.

➤ Travel teaches kids to take pleasure from exploring the natural world—watching a tide pool, collecting pine cones to make forest dolls, rolling down grassy hillsides, seeing an eagle hunt.

➤ Kids learn about other cultures by exposure to them; observing a tribal pow wow in New Mexico, staying in a home in Ireland, visiting a pottery workshop in Mexico, or buying fresh hot tortillas at a *tortilleria* in Baja.

➤ If an extended trip is not possible, take your child to a

local ethnic market and check out a culture-appropriate video from the library.

➤ When traveling, children quickly learn that their favorite foods are not available everywhere, and that some of their favorite foods may indeed be considered disgusting by others—and vice versa. Most kids will try new foods and abandon picky eating habits. Before your trip talk to your children about how food will be different.

➤ You will find that one benefit of travel is to get children away from excessive TV watching. On the other hand, watching TV in a foreign land can be a great way to learn a language and absorb a thing or two about the culture you are visiting.

➤ For really picky eaters, consider offering the child a coin in the local currency for every new food they try. Is this a bribe? Yes!

➤ Pack a small magnetic checker or chess board, backgammon or mancala set, cards, and dominos for family tournaments. On travel days or during rainy weather you may experience long periods of confinement that wouldn't occur at home.

_____ ⭒ _____

We have to show our children how the world turns outside their own back-yards, and travel is the BEST private education we can provide. That is what we have decided to do for our kids—send them to public school and spend the money we would have used for private education on travel. This ranges from the pure fun of Hawaii or Disneyworld to exploring the Yucatan and Belize, and educational visits to Washington, D.C. and New York City.

◆

Martha Dundon, 43, children's librarian

II

$\mathscr{S}$AVORING AND $\mathscr{S}$URVIVING $\mathscr{I}$NFANTS AND $\mathscr{T}$ODDLERS

If your whole world is upside down and joy and cheer are far
from you, romp for an hour with a child and see if his laughter
and faith are not veritable sign posts on the Road to Happiness.

—Gladys Harvey-Knight

YOUR PACE AND OUTLOOK on the world changes with
infants and toddlers in tow. To see the world through the
eyes of a small child is a reawakening of the child within
you. However, when traveling with little ones, planning,
packing, and patience become critical. If you forget certain
paraphernalia, such as an
ample supply of diapers, wet
wipes, pacifier, favorite
teddy bear, or your sense of
humor, the consequences
can be unpleasant.

We dragged our first
child with us all over the
country, continuing to travel
in the same manner as when
we were childless. Ten years
later, our most vivid memories of a trip to Alaska are
not the soaring bald eagles
or foraging grizzly bears, or
snow-covered Mt. McKinley

*I always carry our pediatri-
cian's phone number when we
travel. Once on vacation I
called across the country and
described my child's earache. I
gave the doctor the phone number of a pharmacy located
nearby and she called in our
usual prescription. It saved us
anxiety, a day of hassles, and
visiting an unfamiliar doctor.*

◆

*Elizabeth Rigby, 28,
interior decorator*

viewed on a clear day; no, what we remember are sleepless nights (our baby did not adjust to a different hotel room every night) and meals eaten alone, as one parent paced with our crying baby outside the restaurant. Should we have left her at home? No. We loved having her with us and we learned from the experience.

Traveling with infants teaches you one lesson: surrender. Give in. Keep your travel plans simple. We eventually learned that the easiest way for us to travel with our young children was to rent a cottage or cabin and to stay in one place. We limited our travel time to the journey of getting there and returning. Everyone was happier. Once everyone adjusted to our new environment and began to sleep and eat on a normal schedule again, we relished our free time to play with and savor our children.

Many families travel internationally with their infants and toddlers and I admire them. What a delight it is to have people of other cultures hold and admire your little ones, reaching out to you as a family. Motherhood is a universal connection and many times traveling with your baby or young

Breast-feed babies during take off and landing—it helps prevent pressure problems and ear pain. If your baby is not a nursing baby, offer a bottle, pacifier, or lollipop. The sucking action relieves pressure on the inner ear.

◆

Katy Koontz, 38, freelance travel writer

Don't over-schedule your time, or over-estimate the staying power of yourself or your young ones! Depending on their ages, your kids might well enjoy the simple pleasures of a hot tub back at the hotel more than standing in line for a ride at Disneyland. You might too.

◆

Janet Fullwood, 44, travel editor

child leads to an instant invitation into people's hearts and lives. Whether you travel far or near to home, here are some universal tips that will enhance your journey.

TIPS

➤ Proper equipment is essential. Consider the environment to which you are traveling. Strollers are great for cities. Child carriers (frontpacks/backpacks) work better on beaches, in rural areas with uneven pavement, and in large crowds.

➤ Bring your own carseat for the journey if you are renting a car. Most rental agencies can't guarantee one. The one you bring from home will also give your child a sense of familiarity.

➤ Arrange for cribs ahead of time. Some hotels have a limited number.

➤ Everyone becomes dehydrated when traveling. Take along a water bottle for each child filled with their favorite drink. Dilute juices and avoid artificially sweetened drinks as they often increase thirst rather than reduce it. Make sure to do a leak check before it goes into their backpacks. Include a large bottle of water for yourself.

_____ ⋰⋰⋰ _____

The first thing that went into my suitcase for any trip was a child-rearing book by Penelope Leach, Your Baby and Child. I could look up symptoms to see if they were serious, check to see if my infant should be eating strawberries at six months, how to counteract jet lag, and more. That book was my friend and reassurance far from home. I also noted phone numbers of our pediatrician, home pharmacy, and poison control center on the inside of the front cover.

◆

Susan Brady, 38, production supervisor

➤ When each child is old enough, they should have a backpack that they fill with favorite toys, books, or stuffed animals. Before departure, be sure they have included essential travel items, and that they have left the pet turtle or mouse at home.

➤ If you want to leave town and funds are low, contact the university in the area where you will be going. Some may rent you a dorm room at nominal fee during summer.

➤ If you can afford it, get connecting rooms. You will be amazed at how pleasant it is to close the door on your children after a long day, and enjoy hard-earned privacy.

➤ Consider using a backpack so that you have your hands free to hold onto your child when you are in crowded airports, amusement parks, or museums.

➤ One joy of traveling with infants is their portability and babies love to be held. They will cooperate and sleep more if you use a chest-style carrier to tote them in.

➤ A small plastic bucket for each child offers younger children on a car trip easy access to a few favorite toys and pocket-sized books.

➤ If you are driving a van, set up a potty chair

I combine visits to parks with museums and restaurants so my child can escape from the backpack or stroller to run and play with other children. The Luxembourg Gardens in Paris was a fantasy land of pigeons and pony rides, Punch and Judy puppet shows and carousels. The Gardens tired him out so much that he slept while I enjoyed a meal and a glass of Bordeaux.

◆

Lisa Alpine, 43, writer

during potty training days. It really does come in handy and cuts out a lot of emergency stops.

➤ Plan to dine early. If the restaurant accepts reservations, call in advance, even for a very early dinner. There may be lots of other families planning to have an early dinner too. If the restaurant doesn't accept reservations, arrive before the peak hours to avoid long waits. Carry quiet toys, crayons, and paper.

> *When my husband and I drove across the U.S. with our four small boys (all under the age of six), we had great success by mimicking our normal routine. Each "older" boy brought his favorite stuffed friend, pillow, and blanket. I began sleeping the babies in porta-cribs a week before departure, so that they were able to sleep in their own bed at any hotel or relative's house.*
>
> ◆
>
> *Brenda Davis, 37, full-time mother of four*

➤ Plan the day's activities keeping in mind the baby's normal schedules for feedings, awake, and nap times. They can't keep up with an adult pace. Whenever possible, let them eat and go to bed at their regular meal and bed times.

➤ Kids love room service. They think ordering and eating in the room, watching a good movie is better than any restaurant. This is a good way for you to relax occasionally. Many hotels now offer kids' favorites like pizza on the room service menu.

➤ Parents or adults traveling together should spell each other of child care duties so each person can have time alone. Dad takes one afternoon, mom takes another, and maybe hire a babysitter to have at least one adult night out.

➤ Unscented baby diaper wipes can also serve as hand and face wipes for the whole family, as well as cool off foreheads, wash away blood and dirt from scrapes and scratches, clean up spills, and spiff up sand toys.

➤ Carry a spray bottle of a 1:10 dilution of bleach and water. You can spray the public toilet seats with it before little hands touch all those germs.

III

$\mathscr{W}$EAVING $\mathscr{M}$EMORIES
WITH $\mathscr{S}$CHOOL-$\mathscr{A}$GE
$\mathscr{C}$HILDREN

"I think," said Christopher Robin, "that we ought to eat all our provisions now, so we won't have so much to carry."

—*A. A. Milne*

MANY MOTHERS TELL ME the grade school years are some of the best years for family travel. I agree with them, although I hope to travel with my children all my life. It is wonderful to travel with children who are past the toddler stage and yet still pre-teen. They love airports, they love eating, they love treats, they love to learn, they love being with you, and will usually listen to you, and they have a sense of wonder about our planet and nature. They're more cooperative than babies and more enthusiastic than many a teenager.

Traveling with my children I have met more local people, other mothers, grandmothers, and families than when I have traveled with friends or my husband. As a family, we are more

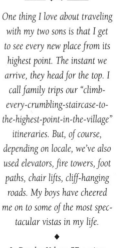

One thing I love about traveling with my two sons is that I get to see every new place from its highest point. The instant we arrive, they head for the top. I call family trips our "climb-every-crumbling-staircase-to-the-highest-point-in-the-village" itineraries. But, of course, depending on locale, we've also used elevators, fire towers, foot paths, chair lifts, cliff-hanging roads. My boys have cheered me on to some of the most spectacular vistas in my life.

♦

Jo Broyles Yohay, 57, writer

approachable, especially now that my children are old enough to play or talk to other kids. The presence of children gives strangers of all ages a reason to strike up a friendly conversation with you. School-age kids meet contemporaries easily, even if there is a language barrier.

> ───── ⁂ ─────
>
> *If I'm visiting a museum with my young children, I go to the gift shop first. I let them choose half a dozen postcards, then we enter the museum for a scavenger hunt to find what is shown on the postcards.*
>
> ♦
>
> *Jasmine Harris, 33, waitress*

At the same time, at this age they don't always need other kids around to be happy and fulfilled. On a recent vacation to British Columbia in the Pacific Northwest we navigated hundreds of miles north from Vancouver toward Alaska through inlets and fjords to where the wild things are—bald eagles, whales, dolphins, seals, bears, glaciers and cascading waterfalls. Cruising through desolate wilderness, with no roads, no phones, few settlements or people, we encountered no other young people for weeks. For days we had no contact with anyone outside the family. Were our kids (ages six and nine at the time) bored? No.

My children found pleasure in the simplest activities— reading and drawing, baking chocolate chip cookies, making windchimes out of tin cans and milk cartons, playing Monopoly, competing in domino tournaments, exploring tidepools and beaches to find the biggest and the smallest purple starfish, collecting oysters on the rocks, or juggling potatoes and lemons. Thanks to our kids we learned how to find, identify, and understand the behavior of jellyfish, starfish, anemone, whales, and birds of prey. Careful planning and packing gave us numerous options for rainy day activities. Most importantly, we learned that we could have a marvelous trip, just the four of us, without the company of peers.

And another thing—I always keep a trip diary. Although I may miss a day or two here and there, I write about more than the places we have visited. I record funny stories, songs, expressions, slang, or jokes that the kids tell at meals. I urge each child to contribute drawings, descriptions, or stories. This gives them a chance to spout off. Shortly after the vacation, they love to reread what they and their siblings have written about the trip, themselves and each other.

> ___ ⚶ ___
>
> *We'll always remember Mt. Vernon, George Washington's home. We went there when we were really little. There was a big white house overlooking the Potomac River and a cake covered with lard on the dining room table. The guide had a funny way of saying "In the ti-iii-iime of George Washington..." before every sentence, which we still imitate when we want to make each other laugh.*
>
> ◆
>
> *Andrea, Noelle, and Mariele O'Reilly, 12, 11, and 9, students*

TIPS

➤ It is helpful to set expectations for a vacation prior to departure. Discuss how things will be different where you are going such as food, entertainment, toilets, language, long travel days, periods of "down time." Children are more agreeable if they know what to expect and are prepared.

➤ Prepare your children in advance with books, videos, brochures and anything that will make them feel more familiar with the place they are traveling. Let them do the research in the library or on the Internet.

➤ Listening to foreign language tapes and watching foreign movies before traveling is helpful for children to understand what to expect in dress, language, and the environment of a foreign country.

➤ When planning your vacation, consider resorts with family programs. Hyatts, Westins, and Club Med are but a few that have these. Don't assume that because one resort in a chain has a good program that others will. Call ahead and speak to someone involved with children's recreation.

> _I explain to my daughters (ages eight and ten) how many people are involved in making our flights safe and pleasant. They in turn show their appreciation by drawing pictures and writing thank you notes to the pilots, stewards and stewardesses. This teaches them to be respectful and gracious, plus it can occupy a good amount of time._
>
> ◆
>
> _Michelle James, 35, critical care nurse manager_

➤ Kids love to have their own money to spend on souvenirs. Talk about where they will have opportunities to buy things, so they can plan ahead. For instance, does the area you're traveling to have any special kind of crafts? This is also a great way to teach adding and subtraction, saving and spending.

➤ Remind your child often (both at home and on vacation) of the "buddy system." No one should go anywhere—outhouse, playhouse, beach—without a buddy, whether that is a sibling, parent, or friend.

➤ Games such as "I spy" can be adapted to different age levels and don't require equipment. "I spy a bird." The next person must say "I spy...." and the thing that they spy must begin with the ending letter of the word said by the first person. Example: "I spy a door." Response, "I spy a road." There are numerous variations to this thinking game, limited only by your imagination.

➤ Cloud formations are fun to look at from the car, and describing the way they look can be lots of fun. Reading the speed limit signs and the highway number signs presents a challenge to youngsters. Older children can be taught to keep a tally of different colors of cars, trucks, and vans. A pencil and paper are all the tools one needs.

➤ Restaurant meal times on the road with small children can be stressful. If you can, plan for lunch in a park or rest stop where the kids can let off steam and help you get the meal together. A Coleman stove and a rest stop can make a breakfast of toast and eggs a simple, inexpensive—and memorable—affair.

➤ Have your children memorize the name of your hotel. Give them a hotel business card to keep in their pocket.

➤ When the inevitable question arises—what should we do now?—remember that kids love animals (think zoos, aquariums, discovery or natural history museums), parks (play structures, hiking trails and picnic areas) and water (lakes, beaches, pool, water slides) and your attention (read or tell stories from when you were a child, play board games such as Yahtzee, checkers, or dominoes). And remember, it's ok to be bored.

➤ There are numerous places to visit and enjoy that are nominal in cost, are educational, and also fun. Children enjoy doing, touching and participating as actively as possible. A trip to the country fair, a farm, or any type of festival where things are going on will entertain and educate. Going to a nearby farm to pick apples, peaches, or berries is high on a child's list of fun things to do because it is a "hands on" activity.

> A trip to a construction site is fascinating for even the youngest child. Machines that go, move earth, and dig holes are awesome. Consider doing things that are not in season. A ride on a ski lift in summer is quite an experience and far less expensive and less crowded than at the height of the ski season. Likewise, check out motels that offer indoor swimming privileges to non-guests for a modest fee during their off season.

> Meals are rarely available or served when my kids are hungry. Carry nutritious, stick-to-your-ribs snacks such as granola bars, raw carrots, raisins, and apples.

> Make sure that the entire family eats raw fruits and vegetables. Drink water, water, water. Constipation is never fun, and especially not while traveling.

> Buy postcards in the airport or in gift shops and bring stationery. Travel time is great for writing to pen pals, friends or grandparents.

When I got out there in the waves with my son and boogie-boarded alongside him, asking his advice on technique since this was my first time, the division between us—a 40-year-old woman and an 11-year-old boy—evaporated and he had a glint of pride in his eye when we both waded to shore with sand in our hair.

♦

Lisa Alpine, 43, writer

➤ Encourage your kids to wear bright colored tops so they are more visible in a crowd.

➤ Kids need lots of physical activity. Carry action toys with you at all times, like a frisbee, inflatable beach ball, tennis ball, or impromptu sports games.

➤ Take luggage wheels on every kind of trip. Then you can haul backpacks and carry-on luggage through airports, train stations, and bus depots, or goodies to the beach.

I bring either a leather toy called an "Un-Ball" or a "koosh-ball" to play with at airports and train stations. These are better than even the softest of round balls because they don't roll when they land (which can easily disturb others), and are easy for small hands or the grown up oaf to catch. It makes transportation delays easier to bear, for both adults and children.

◆

Jasmine Harris, 33, waitress

IV

ADVENTURES WITH YOUR TEENAGERS

If you have a person, understand them or perceive them really and deeply at any one instant in their lives, you have them forever.

—*Anne Morrow Lindbergh*

———◆———

A FRIEND IN NEW YORK, Jo Yohay, told me a story about an adventure she shared with her teenage son, a veteran backpacker and naturalist: "We signed on as volunteers for an expedition to study monkeys on the island of Grenada in the Caribbean. Wearing hiking boots and field pants, mother and son flew south alongside straw-hatted sunseekers on their way to beach bungalows. Our destination: a dorm-style field station where we'd sleep on bunks and wash out muddy socks in a worn-out sink. What I loved was the chance it offered us to be equals—not in the usual parent-child context but as team members, ready to roll up our sleeves and learn side by side."

Jo found a trip that appealed to her son's interests in the natural world. Like Jo, you can tailor your vacation to who your teen is becoming. Spend time researching their current interests. If your daughter is

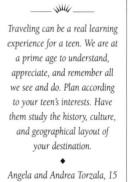

Traveling can be a real learning experience for a teen. We are at a prime age to understand, appreciate, and remember all we see and do. Plan according to your teen's interests. Have them study the history, culture, and geographical layout of your destination.

◆

Angela and Andrea Torzala, 15 and 13, home school students

fascinated with military hardware, take her to an Air Force base or a military museum. If she is entranced with fashion, take her to Paris, Milan, or New York. If your son is interested in marine life, get certified together and go on a scuba diving trip. Make it a surprise trip. This is an especially wonderful idea for graduation presents and gives you the opportunity to spend time with them when they are approaching the age when they will be leaving the nest.

An active vacation is a good choice for teen travel as it directs their bountiful energy, and provides many opportunities to learn new outdoor skills. Such adventures will challenge everyone and give you and your teens a chance to reconnect. Consider wilderness pack trips (with horses, llamas, mules, or backpacks), river rafting adventures (the Grand Canyon and Salmon River in Idaho are worth the splurge), volunteer vacations, or African safaris. See the "Resources and References" chapter for organizations that offer these trips.

When I was a teenager and thought I knew it all I didn't

———— ⚜ ————

I've gone to Tijuana for the past two summers. The first year I was part of a team that built a house for a family that was living in a shack made of cardboard, metal, and scraps of wood and plastic. Their gratitude for the house we built made me so glad I had given up my other summer plans. The second year, we stopped at the house we'd built the summer before. To our amazement, the family had moved back into their shack and turned the small house into a church! Their friends and neighbors had all worked together to build pews and a pulpit to furnish the church. This taught me an unforgettable lesson: these people, who had so little, gave to others out of their own need. Just think of all I could do with what I have!

◆

*Tim Williams, 15,
high school student*

33

want to travel with my family. I wanted to do exactly what my peers were doing. An elderly relative set the stage for my next decade by counseling me with these words: "Finish your education, get a job, save your money and travel on your own. Only after you have done these things should you consider settling down. If you don't have these adventures while you are young and single, you'll regret your lost opportunities all your life. Try to go overseas on an exchange program. Apply for all scholarships and grants. Life comes in CANS. Put CAN'T in a bottle and throw it away. Give yourself the gift of seeing the world. Because then and only then, the dowry you bring to your marriage will be one of inner strength and it will surpass any dowry of family money, lineage, or prestige. You will be a different person, filled with confidence and the knowledge that you can conquer anything. Then you will be ready to shoulder the responsibilities and joys of marriage, motherhood, and career." I took her advice to heart and in the end I did exactly as she counseled. And she was right.

> *I get to talk with my parents more when we travel. It's not like everyday life, when I'm going to school, am so busy with activities that I have no time to sit down and talk. There are usually no negative things on vacation— it is all good.*
>
> ◆
>
> *Renee Zalles, 14, student*

TIPS

➢ When traveling to several different locations try to stay four to five days in one place, so your teens have time to adjust to it and find their way around the immediate vicinity of where you are staying. Then they get a feeling of orientation and independence.

➤ Be aware of what your teenagers are studying in school and include historic tours which will make their studies come alive.

➤ Teens without siblings can sometimes be happier if they take a friend on trips. They always have a "buddy" to do things with, which also translates into safety in numbers and happier kids. Arrange in advance with the other child's parents who will pay for what, and make sure your child's friend knows your rules. Do a dry run by having them stay a weekend at your home.

_____ ⧜ _____

Be sure to participate when your children are selecting colleges. This is a chance to bond, to open new communication. As you tour campuses and do interviews, you will realize that this is one trip where you have the same focus, the same itinerary, and the same goals, a noncontroversial trip with real quality time together. We remember these trips as being among our best. On the other hand, perhaps my worst trip was traveling with our sons to drop them off at college. You think you are so ready to have them leave home, but when the moment comes, it's so painful. It is a passage you can never be totally prepared for. Your life changes forever once they're gone.

◆

Shelby Brough, 51, traveler

➤ If your teens take a long time in the bathroom, remind them that on your trip, sharing a bathroom may require them to be extra considerate.

➤ Have your teens teach you things along the way. They are at an age when they have accumulated wisdom of their own and often have skills they can pass on to us.

➤ Roll up your sleeves and share a volunteer vacation with your teenager. Dozens of non-profit groups offer fascinating trips for paying volunteers both in the U.S. and abroad. They run the gamut of scientific, environmental, educational or social-service expeditions. Because group leaders are on hand to teach skills and monitor progress, volunteer vacations offer a unique opportunity for parent and child to participate as equal learners on a team.

> *I like being with my family more on trips than in everyday life. At home I don't really want to be with my family but when we travel somewhere else I want to be with them because it's more interesting. I don't care about being out with my friends anymore. I am having fun right where I am.*
>
> ◆
>
> Sarah Smith, 16,
> high school student

➤ Consider having each teen bring a personal cassette or CD player with headphones and extra batteries. Agree before departure on where, when, and how often they may plug in.

➤ When your children reach puberty, there's a good chance they will begin to think about one thing most of the time: the opposite sex. They will enjoy their vacation more if they can meet other kids. This is a difficult age, and this is a very good time to practice the art of listening.

> *Recognize that "traveling with Mom" may not be every kid's ideal—cut them plenty of slack, talk about it.*
>
> ◆
>
> Ann Zwinger, 60+, author, poet

➤ If you are traveling abroad with a teenage girl, this is a good time to talk about the many different hues and cons of sexual predators.

➤ Encourage your teen to plan a family day trip—from where to go, what to do, and what to eat. Relax and enjoy it! Soon they may be booking a family trip abroad.

➤ Spread out your long road trips when your kids are young. Many families discover that by the time their kids become teens they are burnt out and refuse to do car trips anymore.

➤ If you are in a safe place and you trust your teens' common sense, give them the freedom to explore. Be sure they take the name, address, and phone number of your accommodations and they know their curfew and customs.

I remember traveling to Europe with my daughter when she was 16. I quickly learned I couldn't drag her around by the hair! So I gave in. I let her sleep until noon while I ran around on my own. We'd have lunch together and tour the rest of the day and evening. She would stay up till 3 a.m. reading if she wanted and eat at McDonalds sometimes. Her idea of a vacation in Italy was sleeping in and shopping for a leather jacket. She returned to Italy later in life and saw the museums and fountains she'd missed.

◆

Christina Wilson, 53, outdoor adventurer

V

$\mathcal{M}$AMA $\mathcal{T}$RAVELS $\mathcal{A}$LONE WITH THE $\mathcal{K}$IDS

Adopt the pace of nature: Her secret is patience.
—*Ralph Waldo Emerson*

TRAVELING ALONE with your children is similar to a demanding physical workout. Just as it can be hard to motivate yourself to go to the gym or put on the jogging shoes and hit the trail, preparing for travel alone with kids can seem equally daunting. The workout, like the trip isn't so tough after you get started and you'll feel so good when it's over. The rewards of traveling alone with your kids are like a huge shot of endorphines—a feeling of power, strength, and control. Everyone becomes closer to each other on the trip and you'll return with renewed self-confidence.

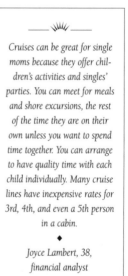

Cruises can be great for single moms because they offer children's activities and singles' parties. You can meet for meals and shore excursions, the rest of the time they are on their own unless you want to spend time together. You can arrange to have quality time with each child individually. Many cruise lines have inexpensive rates for 3rd, 4th, and even a 5th person in a cabin.

♦

Joyce Lambert, 38, financial analyst

Every summer when school is out, my daughters and I take off for our annual mother/daughter get-away. We usually go camping because as a child I learned to feel comfortable in the woods and it is to the woods or wilderness that I return for peace, solace, and rejuvenation. So I take my kids into the great outdoors so they will learn the meditative and healing effects of nature. We pitch our tent, collect firewood, carry cooking water, and explore the woods. After dark we build a huge camp fire, roast marshmallows, watch the glowing embers, and search the heavens for shooting stars. The kids return home with great memories and more outdoor skills. I return, more at peace with myself, and with a long-lasting conviction that I can take my kids by myself and travel anywhere! You don't have to be a single mom to be a mom traveling alone with kids. You don't have to stay home because you don't have an adult companion.

Some of the gutsiest women I know and admire are single mothers who travel with their children all the time, almost everywhere. In Fairlawn, Ohio, a single mom told me her story of driving alone to Alaska with her 3-year-old daughter and camping for two months. I was humbled by her courage and she was still amazed by her adventures. And these stories are not unusual. I applaud every mother who has taken her children camping or traveling on her own. Kids gain respect and pride for their mom and her abilities.

———— ⚲ ————

Four years ago I traveled alone with my 12-year-old daughter to visit our 95-year-old grandmother. My husband always handles the logistics of our family trips. This was new for me to travel alone with a child. When we encountered severe weather and plane cancellations, my daughter became very nervous. When I asked her what was wrong, she replied. "Mom, can you handle this?" I was stunned. I realized at that moment that moms need to let kids know they are capable!

♦

Suzanne Smith, 41,
mother of four

TIPS

➤ If you're driving, get a map and study it before you go. Write out explicit directions from Point A to Point B and keep that paper in the front seat with you. Glancing at those directions while driving is a lot easier than looking at a map. If your kids are old enough to read, they can help (and feel important) by reading the directions to you.

➤ If you can afford it, consider traveling on the sleeping car of a train. You are free from the stress of driving and the excitement of riding the rails will make lasting memories for you and your children. Security is generally quite good, meals are taken care of and porters can sometimes help you with overload situations. Day trips on Amtrak can also be fun and affordable. Pack a picnic lunch!

➤ On the first day of a long road trip, leave home before dawn. By the time your children are fully awake, you can stop for breakfast, teeth-brushing and a stretch. You will have one hundred or so miles out of the way

> _Traveling alone with my son is one of the best ways to get to know him; it gives us both a chance to see each other in new and often difficult situations and environments. As a single mom, I think my son gained new respect for me. He saw me behaving bravely in difficult situations. In Mexico he watched me assertively negotiate in a foreign language and take charge—ordering tickets, meals and finding lodging. In places where English was not spoken, he was utterly dependent on me in a way he is not at home. He came back looking at me through different eyes._
>
> ◆
>
> _Pamela Michael, 45, writer_

and everybody will feel like the trip is just beginning. Finish the day early at a hotel with a pool. Never underestimate the power of water to reset whatever it is that makes us tick.

➤ Encourage your children to participate in all aspects of your trip beginning with the pre-trip planning. Once on the road, give an older child the responsibility of being the navigator, encourage another to be the feeder, to provide snacks and drinks and another to tell stories. They can switch roles and you can enjoy the trip more when you aren't always guide, porter, feeder and map reader.

➤ Individual identification for each child is a must! Their ID can be a simple business card with their name and your name and phone number on it. They

_____ ⋇ _____

I've found that driving long distances alone with my kids can be a challenge. My boys are very active (ages 6 and 10) and don't do well for long periods in the car. So I alternate several hours of driving with several hours of activities. Recently we did an eight-hour drive in two days. The first day we traveled four hours and stopped at a place with a waterpark; the next day we swam at the hotel pool until noon and then took off. It works for us.

◆

Joan Corbett, 51, executive, nonprofit organization

_____ ⋇ _____

My mother has always worked, and raised nine children alone. After I graduated from college, I saved all summer to surprise her with a ticket to Ireland. International travel was new to both of us. We laughed and learned together all the way across the land of our heritage. It was the beginning of many subsequent adventures.

◆

Brenda Davis, 37, full-time mother of four

should carry it inside their packs, in purses, or sewn into their clothing.

➤ You have only two hands and one back, so check all luggage except that which contains the essentials.

➤ Ask the flight attendants, when they are not serving a meal, to watch your kids when you need to use the bathroom or just walk around the plane and take a short break. It's for the sake of other passengers as well as the kids.

➤ Traveling with children it is important to be cognizant of the hour of sunset. All over the world, towns which are filled with activity during the day can empty out once darkness descends. Plan your day so you return to your accommodations before dark.

➤ When traveling across a border, or through immigration to numerous countries, such as Mexico, single mothers are required to show a notarized letter of permission from the child's other parent. If the other parent is deceased, you will need proof of death. While this may seem to represent bureaucratic excess, there is a good reason for it—divorced or estranged spouses have been known to kidnap disputed children and take them abroad.

➤ When you arrive in a new location consider taking an organized tour. It will give you an overview of the city and a better idea of where you may want to spend your time.

➤ You'll be surprised how accommodating and eager strangers can be to lend a hand when you ask for help. Other mothers often know what you are going through and are just waiting for your invitation to assist.

➤ Always go last. The kids should hike ahead of you on the trail or enter the plane before you. If your children are ahead of, and behind you, it is easy for one of them to take off in any direction without you noticing. Continually make a head and luggage count.

VI

ON THE ROAD
WITH GRANDMA
AND GRANDPA

If we had known grandkids were so much fun,
we'd have had them first.

—*Inscription on a senior citizen's cap*

GRANDPARENTS TODAY are staying healthy and active longer than past generations and many have enough excess income to travel. More and more intergenerational families are taking to the road, the skies, the seas, and the rails...and loving it. Everyone is enriched by cross-generation bonding, grandparent mentoring, and different generations learning and exploring together.

Not surprisingly, tour companies, outdoor outfitters, and Elderhostel are offering a wide variety of trips ranging from week-long rafting adventures on the San Juan River in Southern Utah to American Indian Culture trips with Navajo-guided jeep tours of Canyon de Chelly in Arizona.

My children and I are fortunate to have traveled a great deal with my parents—from sliding down sand dunes at Cape Cod to hiking trips in the Colorado

City day trips are a good way to get a break from each other. While grandma is learning all about the history of the city on a bus tour, I rented roller skates and buzzed around Golden Gate Park in San Francisco.

◆

Joanne Richards, 32, nurse

Rockies and skipping rocks on the shores of Lake Tahoe. We never hesitate to join grandma and grandpa, or ask them to join us anywhere, anytime. Sometimes my husband can come, but with less vacation time than I, he usually urges us to go on our own. Soon my children will be old enough to go on their own too.

Traveling with grandma is a great way to learn about your roots. My grandmother took me to Prince Edward Island when I was young to show me where her parents were born. We went to the cemetery and she was related to almost everyone buried there. She told me who they were and she went back generations. It was a trip I will never forget and I hope to take my grandchildren there someday.

◆

Sarah Reyna, 28,
mother and wife

Grandchildren bring out the child in the grandparents. Grandpa runs along the beach flying kites with his grandchildren and grandma catches butterflies and makes insect gardens in terrariums. They share the things they knew and loved as kids: riding bikes, reading and being read to, baking cookies, fishing, sewing doll clothes. Grandparents give children a unique perspective on their family history, are gentle mentors, and alternative teachers. Everyone benefits from bridging the gap.

TIPS

➢ Discuss homesickness before they leave and assure them when and how often you will call.

➢ Remind your children that grandma and grandpa are to be treated with respect and kindness.

➢ Review for grandparents the routines, restrictions, and special habits of your children (especially if they haven't seen them in a while) such as bedtime, amount of candy or dessert permitted, or reading time before lights go out.

➢ Grandparents, parents, and kids need down time as well as time to visit or play with their peers. Take children to a park, beach or a pool so they can meet others their own age. Grandparents need a break to take a nap, read, or talk on the phone. Everyone will be happier if each generation has time off.

➢ Encourage grandparents to share stories of the "olden days." Relate historic events to their grandchildren's studies, e.g., first Model T, moon landing, Woodstock, and so forth.

➢ Visiting grandparents can afford children the opportunity to ask questions about mom or dad when they were young. This can create a strong link between past and present. Try the following theme: "Let me tell you a story about when your (mother or father) was bad." Children take special delight in hearing about the behavior of their parents, especially the naughty stuff.

➢ On their return, remind your children to write thank you notes to the grandparents and perhaps send them a mini-photo

I remember going to Aghadoe Cemetery where my Grandpa is buried. It is a very pretty place overlooking the Lakes of Killarney in County Kerry, Ireland. I was sad as I picked wildflowers but I was glad to be there too. We said a prayer next to the grave with my Grandma. We also met one of my Grandpa's boyhood friends who was there to visit his relative's grave.

◆

Mariele O'Reilly, 9, student

album of the photographs taken on the trip.

➤ When your young children travel to visit grandma or grandpa without you, pack a special good luck charm, like a family picture, in their bags to remind them of you and curb homesickness.

➤ On a car trip, pack cassette players and numerous music and book tapes so kids and adults can each listen to their own music while others enjoy silence or conversation.

➤ Inform grandkids of any medical conditions grandparents may have so that they are prepared if an emergency should arise. They should also know where important medicine is kept while traveling.

_____ ⋰⋰⋰ _____

Grandparents can acquaint their grandchildren with their ancestors while on vacation together. We tell stories of past generations, when they emigrated to American, where they lived and who were their children. We call these sessions "And they were great and strong." It instills pride in children to learn how their ancestors endured hardship and prevailed.

◆

*Ruth Bond, 79,
retired school teacher*

_____ ⋰⋰⋰ _____

My grandmother and I began traveling abroad when she turned 81. Over the next four years we visited 40 countries. People would often tell her she was lucky to have such a capable granddaughter to accompany her, but I'd always insist that I was the lucky one.

◆

*Chelsea George, 35,
entrepreneur*

➤ Let grandma or grandpa set rules she or he are comfortable with, (like bedtime or curfew) even if they are different from yours.

➤ Take lots of pictures and videos. A framed photograph of grandkids and grandparents together on vacation makes a wonderful Mother's Day, Father's Day, or holiday present.

➤ Keep a journal of your travels with your children and their grandparents. Encourage both the kids and the seniors to make entries or drawings in the diary every few days. You will treasure this family history when the older generation is gone.

VII

MAMA TRAVELS WITHOUT THE FAMILY

Momma not happy,
Ain't nobody happy.
—*Caribbean Saying*

———

WHEN I TRAVEL BY MYSELF, whether it is for business or pleasure, for one night close to home, or for a two week safari, I return renewed, recharged, and recommitted to my family. Traveling away from family members gives me time to appreciate them, to focus on the important issues in our lives, to evaluate my priorities, to muse about the passages in my life, the amazing changes in my children's' lives, and to have a break.

Travel has always given me a way to break with tradition, to ignore gender specific roles, cross boundaries, push my limits, and reaffirm my sense of personal power. As a mother, I find that when I go off on my own for a while, the typical roles we play at home are abandoned. Dad becomes mom, kids become adults and better friends. New rituals develop as dad spoils the kids and does things his way, which I've noticed includes take-out meals, ice cream, videos, and late bedtimes. My absences allow a more intense bonding between my children and their father. And we all appreciate each other more. On the road, as I shed the burden of household responsibilities, I too assume different roles and expand my vision of what is possible.

Sometimes I feel guilty before I leave home to travel for business or pleasure. I worry something may happen to me or them in my absence. I can't leave home unless I feel that my children are safe and well taken care of. To overcome my hesitation I organize excellent childcare, leave household matters in order, and remind myself that a break in routine is good for me and my family. I know from experience I will come back healthier and happier. My guilt and the pain of separation will fade. Because of my passion for travel, I would feel too much a martyr if I stopped traveling completely, if I never took time for myself. If I felt like a martyr I wouldn't make a healthy or happy mom. My patient husband understands and supports me and travels strengthen our relationship.

> *Mothers who travel solo begin to claim the rights of financial independence, leadership qualities, assertiveness, confidence, a sense of self, peer esteem, physical stature, strength, sexual impregnability, and creditability. When a women is empowered with these rights, her societal role is more similarly situated and equal to men. Once she experiences this liberation, travel becomes not just a temporary liberation or personal tonic, but a prescription for social equilibrium.*
>
> ◆
>
> *Martha Dundon, 43, children's librarian*

TIPS

➤ Everyone has a different ideal length of time away from home and your flexibility often depends on the age of your children and your own personality. If you don't travel for business, try to plan an overnight alone or with a friend several times a year. If you do travel for your work, reserve an extra day, or at the least an afternoon of unscheduled time for yourself.

➤ Communicate with home often. The easiest and cheapest way to keep in touch from most countries is via email and faxes. Both are less expensive than making a long distance phone call, and you don't have to deal with time differences. If you receive a fax from home you can keep and reread it. I treasure love letters and children's drawings faxed to me when I travel, and I often share them with fellow travelers.

➤ When your children are young, leave a goodie bag at home with a gift for each child for each day you'll be gone. The present can be as small as a pack of gum or a colorful postcard with a love note on it. Kids look forward to opening a special love present from Mom every day. Some days you may leave an envelope and make it a treasure hunt to find the present. They'll understand when the gifts run out that you'll be home that day.

➤ Make preparations to ease the workload for your family while you are away; stock up on groceries, catch up on laundry, leave the house clean if you can, fix a few frozen meals but don't work yourself into a frenzy.

> _____ \\\\///_ _____
>
> *I will reward myself for the week I took off work to attend my husband's convention in Memphis, the week it took to get the three children ready for camp, and the wet ten days we spent as a family in Pennsylvania with the relatives. I now will go find a table by myself, sprinkled with jacaranda petals, and drink hibiscus tea, and slowly eat mango slices and avocado while I read the new Margaret Atwood novel and try to figure out if the couple at the next table are married to each other. Then I will walk whichever street my sandals take me to and look for the shop with the green hat in the window before taking a siesta. And we'll all like me better when I return home.*
>
> ◆
>
> *Susan Swartz, 40+ newspaper columnist*

➤ When you travel without the kids give yourself the green light to pamper yourself. Pack bubble bath, a bottle of wine, a good book, your favorite music.

➤ Consider an annual getaway with a close friend, sister, or your mother. Trips with other women are powerful times for bonding, healing, and laughter.

➤ Retreats at local monasteries of almost any religious persuasion are spiritually renewing. Think of them as a kind of mental spring cleaning. Soon you will realize this is not a luxury, but like spring cleaning, a necessity.

➤ Keep a journal of your thoughts and record changes in yourself and your children. Distance from your loved ones lends itself to reflection.

➤ Take several small framed pictures of your family to display in your hotel room to help you feel connected to home.

➤ Carry stationery and envelopes in your

I am a stay-at-home mom. I keep telling myself that it is OK to take time to nurture myself. I am always a wife and mother, and I love it...but sometimes it's necessary to get away to re-establish my sense of self.

◆

Sarah Reyna, 27,
mother & wife

After 25 years of marriage and two children, anticipating a divorce, I decided to test myself. I needed to see if I could exist as an "I" when I had always been a "we." I learned I wasn't dead at 52. I learned that I didn't have to have anyone to go with me. I could just go. Through travel, I found a way to redefine myself.

◆

Virginia Barton Brownback, 72,
writer and photographer

carry-on bag so you can catch up on personal correspondence or fax a short note home as soon as you arrive. Receiving a handwritten letter these days is a rare treat.

➤ When planning a break without the family, choose a new destination and activities you probably wouldn't do with them—a bike trip in Ireland, a cooking school in France, a spa in California, sailing school on the coast, or hiking hut-to-hut in the Rockies. Avoid family or romantic resorts where you will be surrounded by children or couples.

> *For those of us afflicted with wanderlust, travel is not negotiable. Without it, I would dry up and die. My husband understands this now, though he was a bit bewildered at first since he doesn't have the same need, is not drawn by the open road as I am. I'm lucky. He supports me to strike off on my own self-confrontational trips from time to time.*
>
> ◆
>
> Jo Broyles Yohay, 52, writer

VIII

TRAVEL COMPANIONS

Through travel we learn to know not only our own world,
but ourselves in a new relationship.

—Seneca

YOUR CHOICE OF TRAVEL COMPANIONS is probably the most important decision you will make for your trip. It will set the tone and make or break a great vacation. You may travel with your entire family; including grandparents, babysitter and pets, or you may choose to travel with another family, or just one child, one girlfriend, or your mother.

Whatever your final decision, it should not be made lightly. Consider how well you know the people you are inviting and carefully weigh the pros and cons. I impulsively made such a decision recently to invite another mother and her child to join us on a trip abroad. I thought I knew the woman. We had known each other socially for years. On the trip I realized for the first time not only how different our backgrounds were but also how opposed our approach to parenting was. The accumulated stress between us led her to mount a devastating verbal attack on my 6-year-old on the last

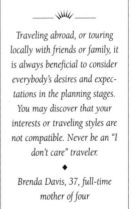

Traveling abroad, or touring locally with friends or family, it is always beneficial to consider everybody's desires and expectations in the planning stages. You may discover that your interests or traveling styles are not compatible. Never be an "I don't care" traveler.

◆

Brenda Davis, 37, full-time mother of four

day, leaving my daughter in tears and our trip in shambles. I now have 20/20 hindsight about what went wrong and why I never should have included her in our vacation. The wrong travel companions will ruin your trip and probably your friendship.

At the other end of the spectrum, we have very close friends with whom we have camped, skied, or backpacked every year for nearly two decades, going back to when we were all single. Both families have children now and our friendship has deepened over the years because of the intimate times we've shared traveling together.

When your children are young, inviting a babysitter or relatives to help gives you some time off but also takes away some of your privacy and adds to your responsibilities. Traveling with another family can assure playmates for your kids and other adults to share the load so you all have more time off.

Today working women travel more for business than in any time in our history. So grown daughters often have frequent flyer miles to share. Women are inviting their mothers to join them on trips. And childhood girlfriends who have not seen each other in decades now have the chance to recapture the fun of their youth planning reunions or trips together.

Not only are women traveling more and more, but they are doing it in dif-

> ___ \\|// ___
>
> *We take most of our vacations with other families. My feeling is both the guys and gals need to get along. Everyone needs to be on the same wavelength as far as what you want out of the vacation. If the parents have the same expectations and set of rules it will work. If one family is strict and the other lenient, the kids will bicker. We won't travel with families that don't set bedtimes for their kids, they are grumpy and the next day is trashed.*
>
> ◆
>
> *Alison Dumont, 43, nurse*

ferent combinations—grown daughter with mother, mothers with maturing daughters, sisters, best girlfriends and female soul mates with each other.

If you are a mom and want to travel, it is no longer an excuse to stay home because you don't have a travel companion. There are women's travel clubs and many organized tour groups catering to women. Another viable option is traveling by yourself. You may begin the trip alone, but you will not stay alone. You will meet many like-minded women out there traveling solo too. Give serious consideration to your travel companions. Above all, don't jump into this decision.

TIPS

➢ When renting a vacation home with other families, split all deposit payments as soon as they are due and put your verbal agreement into a friendly note to the other family con-

---

_\\\\\//_

My sister Marilyn had lived with lung cancer for five years when she decided to take a European vacation with her grown children Brea and Alex, and her husband. By luck, my partner and I had planned a similar vacation at the same time. It all added up to the trip of a lifetime—literally. Marilyn couldn't have taken such a trip even a few months later: the accumulation of lung surgeries, chemotherapy, and radiation had become too debilitating. It was extremely difficult for her. Yet, amazingly, my niece and nephew's memories are mostly of laughing and cherishing the strangeness of a trip abroad—Beavis and Butthead on French TV, the beauty of Bath. The next year Marilyn died, but Brea and Alex remember the gift of that trip as a statement of who their mother was. Marilyn refused to live in her pain, leaving us all with extraordinary memories of a woman who wanted to experience the world with those she loved the most.

◆

*Ellen Elias, 47,
software publicist*

cerning refunds and reimbursement of full payment if one party should cancel. If it is in writing, everything is clear.

> The more families that share a rental home, the less expensive it will be for each party. However, keep in mind that the noise and activity level increases exponentially.

> Traveling with your mother, best friend, or sister, you may find that as much as you enjoy spending time together there are times when it is best to spend time apart. You may consider going with a group where it is easier to occasionally go off and

The hardest and most important thing for me to remember was that this was the family's vacation, first before mine. Whether skiing in Colorado or vacationing in Hawaii, taking care of the children away from home can require different hours, activities, and levels of responsibility. Being flexible and respecting their space was always mirrored back to me. Once, while traveling with my family, I was pleasantly surprised one night when they brought me back dessert from their private dinner. It was a simple thoughtful gesture that helped melt the invisible lines between employee and employer that are sometimes awkward while vacationing abroad.

♦

—Jennifer Leo, 26, writer and former nanny

do your own thing, and not feel guilty. You each will have quality time alone and with each other.

> If you are on a group trip and are assigned a roommate you don't know, it is a good idea to meet before the trip, even over the phone. Then you can discuss who will bring what, such as a hairdryer.

> When you share quarters with a roommate it can be helpful to decide right away who will have which bed

or which side of the sink or closet.

➢ If you include a babysitter in your vacation plans, be very clear about working hours, days off, salary, and expectations while traveling. Pre-trip conversations will help lessen the confusion for the babysitter/nanny/relative joining you for the first time.

➢ What is a vacation for you is not a vacation for your babysitter. Being away from home requires a higher level of safety awareness, as well as energy keeping up with the excited, swimming, running, playing child. Extra energy is also required to deal with the quiet, bored, or homesick child. Ways to show your appreciation of their help include: letting them sleep in one day while you get the kids ready and fed, bring home dessert from your dinner out, give them time to themselves, offer to cook a meal if they're usually doing it, let them make an occasional phone call home to their own family or loved ones.

➢ If you travel and hike with your pet, remember, most medium to large dogs can wear dogpacks and carry their own water and treats on hikes, as well as other small items.

- ➤ While on the road with your dog, it is easier to pack dry dog food in individual, pre-measured baggies. You know how much you need in advance and won't have to pack more than necessary.

- ➤ Train your pet to drink from various sources: water fountains, squirt bottles, hoses. Animals who will only drink out of a bowl may become dehydrated when it is not available.

After an eighteen hour flight to Bangkok everyone in our group had a stranger for a roommate. All we wanted was a good night of sleep. Being prepared can ease your adjustment to a situation like this, such as using a night light for reading, bringing eye shades and ear plugs for yourself and a roommate.

People have different ideas about reading at night to relax, but many of us can't sleep with a light on in the room. Most people are polite and won't ask someone to turn off the light, so come prepared.

◆

Christina Wilson, 53, outdoor adventurer

IX

SAFETY ON THE ROAD

Lifesaving techniques are in themselves a wonderful idea.
What makes some of the safety entrepreneurs notorious,
however, is the pressure they put on mothers to take their
courses and, once in the course, to feel blood terror
over every possible life contingency.

—Sonia Taitz, American writer

SAFETY AND SECURITY FOR THE FAMILY is the number one concern for parents at home, and doubly so when traveling. Accidents happen in familiar environments, but the chances of incidents increase when children are exploring unfamiliar surroundings. It is important to prepare and coach your children about travel and its perils. Explain that they will be seeing new and wondrous things, but they'll need to pay closer attention to the people and objects around them. Help them learn how to recognize and respond to dangerous situations by explaining what they will be likely to encounter, such as busy airports, narrow streets with congested traffic, climates dramatically different from what they're used to, or ocean waves far more powerful than the lake at home. Make it positive so you don't alarm them. Counsel them to trust their instincts and to

When traveling in countries where people drive on the left side of the road, it always takes at least a few days to adjust as a pedestrian to looking to the right for traffic. Remind your children to do this every time you cross the street. And then be careful on your return home when you have to go back to your old ways!

◆

Jasmine Harris, 33, waitress

stop and find you if they have doubts. Playing it safe while traveling requires intuition, common sense, and careful preparation.

Children need to know how to ask for help when they need it and to whom they should turn for help.

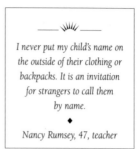

I never put my child's name on the outside of their clothing or backpacks. It is an invitation for strangers to call them by name.

♦

Nancy Rumsey, 47, teacher

As moms, we too must learn to ask for assistance. I am always amazed by the friendliness and help that strangers offer when I ask. The world is often a much friendlier place than we hear about in the media. One of the things that travel teaches us is just how dangerous our own country can be. Children are often revered in countries that have much lower standards of living than ours.

Whenever you ask, "Where is it?" add "Is it safe?" Recently in Washington, D.C., my daughter and I finished dinner and prepared to walk from Union Station to our hotel several blocks away. I asked for advice. Women encouraged us to take a cab, a man said, "No problem, just walk." It is wise to ask more than one source. And always get a second opinion from a woman if the first person you've asked is a man.

Safety is always relative. No matter where you are, you have to concern yourself with protection from criminals, whether they be sexual predators, robbers, pickpockets, or con artists. Talk to your children about the possibilities of encountering such people, being sure to explain that such things happen but that if you're careful they can usually be avoided.

Political unrest can occur even in the most friendly countries, so if your travels take you to places where passions are simmering, be sure to discuss the possibility of demonstrations and what they might mean. You can usually avoid getting caught up in such incidents, but it's important for children to know what to do in these circumstances.

If you're traveling to a place susceptible to natural disasters, such as tropical areas during hurricane season, be sure to know how to respond if a storm blows in. Tell your children what to expect if it appears that there's a threat, and be prepared to abandon your vacation plans and go home if necessary. The old saying, "Better safe than sorry," has been around for generations for good reason.

Similarly, you can't give your children enough guidance concerning water activities. Learning to swim is vital to a child's enjoyment of a full life, but remember that simple swimming lessons don't always work for every child. If your child hates swimming lessons you should find an alternative teacher who can gain the child's trust and keep the experience fun. As long as

—— ＼＼l／／ ——

Make sure your children know how to swim. Enroll them in lessons at an early age, and stick with it, even if they profess not to like the water. We did (she didn't) and now she is the queen of water nymphs.

♦

*Karen Cure, 40+,
editorial director*

—— ＼＼l／／ ——

Teach your children about the behavior of the sea and how to read waves to gauge the safety of beaches. Look for patterns in the waves: if every seventh one is a whopper, be prepared to keep an eye on them. Look for patterns in the sand: deeply sculpted beaches indicate powerful waves and rip tides (often called undertows). And be sure to ask locals about rogue waves: if they occur in the area everyone in your party should play together and keep an eye out for each other.

♦

*Larissa Mendez, 38,
car mechanic*

the process is fun, your child will learn, and in time be a swimmer you can trust in the water.

TIPS

➢ Discuss safety issues with your children before you go. Lay down some travel rules. Explain why things may be different somewhere else and where to go or who to approach if they need to get help. Discuss what phone number they can call for help.

➢ If you haven't taken Red Cross first aid courses, do so. You won't regret it. If you have taken them, find time to take a refresher.

➢ Review what to do if someone gets lost and how important it is not to stray.

➢ Always have a plan and a good map when traveling with your children, or on your own. Be aware of your surroundings and constantly alert to possible danger.

> *Our youngest daughter has a high-pitched scream which can be heard over the noise of any traffic. We encouraged her to use it if she had to, and on a couple of occasions in London and Paris when she was four, she became separated from us, but only briefly, as she announced her location with one astounding crystal-clear shriek.*
>
> ◆
>
> Wenda Brewster, 49, writer

➢ Kids need identification (like dog tags or an ID bracelet) on them at all times in case you get separated. Travel pouches that are worn under clothes are good as long as the child is old enough not to choke on it if it gets caught on something. Many styles of protective passport holders, etc. can be found in travel book stores and specialty travel shops.

➤ Carry an up-to-date and clear photograph of your child(ren). Know their birthmarks and make a list of them to carry with your documents.

➤ If you have small children, teach them their full name, address, and telephone number with area code. Since no one is likely to be at home while you are on vacation they should also memorize another number for emergencies.

➤ Role play the safety game "what would you do if?" Children remember role play with you or their siblings longer than they do lectures.

➤ Make sure you stay in a safe neighborhood in a secure hotel. When you check in, scrutinize the walk from your car to the lobby or your room. Are the outdoor areas well lit? Are you on the ground floor with sliding doors that open onto a public area? It may seem charming to have a room with sliding glass doors that open onto a garden near the pool area until you discover that while you take a shower it is easy for your child to take off to explore. Change rooms if your location seems

When I travel alone with my children, on camping trips and long drives, I take our dog. The added security (and the companionship she gives the kids) more than makes up for the hassle.

◆

Larissa Mendez, 38, car mechanic

My children wear whistles around their necks, to use should they get lost in crowds in big cities, or lost in the woods by running ahead of me.

◆

Shana Ralleigh, 45, retired exotic dancer

inappropriate or unsafe for any reason.

➢ In a hotel, never send a child alone to get ice or soft drinks.

➢ Keep your medications in a safe place when traveling. There are no locked medicine cabinets on the road and children tend to explore everything.

> *I've learned when traveling, especially in developing countries, to avoid swimming where the locals don't swim and walking barefoot on beaches.*
>
> ◆
>
> *Gail Burg, 34, professor*

➢ Avoid being a target for thieves and leave jewelry at home. If possible, don't carry a purse, use a fanny pack or moneybelt. Keep cameras and valuables in locked bags or backpacks and don't leave them in sight in your car.

➢ If you are traveling by car, carry a can of Spare Tire. This product, which is sold under a variety of different names, temporarily inflates flat tires and enables you to drive to a gas station without having to change tires. This may save you hours of aggravation and exposure to road creeps.

➢ When you arrive at theme parks, museums, and other crowded places, select a central meeting area in case you get separated. Counsel your children to approach an employee to ask for help if they are lost. If they need to find you in a crowd, advise them to call you by your first name. There will be lots of other mommies.

➢ Remember, not all dogs are vaccinated. Teach your children to keep their distance, even if they wag their tails. Rabies shots are extremely painful and can botch any vacation. So can getting stitches if the dog bites.

➢ Be aware of the risk you are taking if you travel in taxis or buses without seatbelts.

➢ Know the customs of the country you are visiting. There are some cultures where a female should never make eye contact or friendly gestures towards males. And vice versa for your teenage son who might otherwise ogle the local beauties. This is especially true in Muslim countries, but is by no means restricted to them. Observe carefully and ask questions.

➢ Warn your daughters and sons when traveling overseas to be wary of anyone who asks them to carry a package or drive a car across a border. Innocent young women are especially targeted to be couriers for drug dealers. The young man they meet may be charming and persuasive. Once a package or anything in the vehicle is in her possession, she becomes totally responsible for it. She will be guilty until proven innocent, assessed a huge fine, and may spend time in jails where the living conditions are barbaric. Even in Mexico, if she

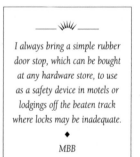

_____ ⚶ _____

I always bring a simple rubber door stop, which can be bought at any hardware store, to use as a safety device in motels or lodgings off the beaten track where locks may be inadequate.

♦

MBB

is convicted of possessing even small amounts of marijuana or cocaine, she'll go to jail.

$\mathscr{S}$ TAYING $\mathscr{H}$ EALTHY

The cure for anything is salt water—sweat, tears, or the sea.
—*Isak Dineson*

———————

IF YOUR CHILD OR COMPANION becomes sick on vacation, your entire trip may be compromised, or at the very least you may spend one or more worrisome days finding doctors and medicine.

Fortunately, only twice on all our travels has a family member been very ill. My memories of those vacations include intense moments of angst, vulnerability, and anger over incompetent doctors who misdiagnosed my children. Children will get sick, so will we. Prevention and planning are the key to good health on the road. On the other hand, illness on a trip or at home provides for closeness, tenderness, growth, and understanding.

Personal physicians often don't have extensive experience or stay up to date on travel medicine. If you are planning a trip to developing countries or off the beaten path, visit a special travelers' clinic. Several HMO's have established travel clinics for their members. Ask your health care provider. Also contact the CDC (Centers for Disease Control) in Atlanta. The CDC receives their medical recommendations from the World Health Organization, (part of the United Nations). The CDC, naturally cautious, offers excellent health recommendations. They have a general phone number for information, (see Resource Section), with a specific extension detailing the latest information about malaria.

Certain health concerns should not be taken lightly. If a

written notice is sent home from your child's day care, or school, informing you that they have been exposed to chicken pox—take it seriously and do not travel until the incubation period is over. Recently a mother had a terrible experience in Hawaii when her child came down with a severe case of chicken pox. The child's face was covered with spots, and there was no way to disguise it. The child was miserable and they wanted nothing more than to fly home. The airline refused to let them fly, and they were denied rooms at hotels, motels and bed and breakfast inns.

What did the woman do? She called every friend she knew in the States and eventually found a friend-of-a-friend who lived in Hawaii who let them stay in their in-law unit in the garden until her child was well enough to travel. An ounce of precaution can save your vacation.

> ——— 〰 ———
>
> *When my son was still crawling age, we went to Bali. He couldn't handle the tropical heat or the black rice pudding and ended up with a high fever and vomiting. We were in a remote village and I had heard horror stories of medical treatment in Indonesia, so I flagged down a truck, handed the driver a $20 bill and told him to take us to the biggest chain hotel on the island, a Hyatt. I went to the front desk, fevered son in my arms, and asked if there were any American doctor guests. The house doctor was a graduate of Harvard Medical School, had practiced ten years in the States and spoke perfect English. I booked a room, received treatment, and within three hours my son was better.*
>
> ◆
>
> —Lisa Alpine, 43, writer

Don't forget that the most common ailment while traveling is a bad stomach. Gastrointestinal problems and diarrhea are usually not life-threatening but they can sure make you miserable. The best ways to avoid the trots are to maintain a good diet, eating reasonably and avoiding especially rich foods the first few days, to drink only beverages you know are safe, and to make sure the food you eat is fresh and well-cooked. These practices are much more important in developing countries where sanitation is suspect, but even in highly developed countries the bacteria may be different from what you're used to at home, so take it easy the first few days. Remember, too, that intestinal disease is far more dangerous for infants and any such illness in a young one should be taken very seriously.

Many moms travel with a panoply of medications to cover just about any eventuality, while others find that simple homeopathic travel kits address many of the health issues that come up. Find what works for you, but most important, remember that the same things that keep you healthy at home will go a long way to keeping you healthy while traveling: get plenty of rest, eat well, and don't overdo it.

> *A day or two before departure on a long trip we all take echinacea. I swear by it as a natural jump start to my immune system. It is so easy to catch viruses in recirculated airplane air, especially when you are rundown. Echinacea, an herbal supplement derived from the North American purple coneflower, is available at most U.S. health food stores. It isn't approved by the FDA, since it's not processed like conventional medicine. Europeans use it all the time when they feel themselves coming down with a cold and it is available at neighborhood pharmacies throughout Western Europe.*
>
> ◆
>
> *MBB*

TIPS

➢ Make sure your vaccinations are up to date. Start getting your shots two months prior to departure. Some immunizations require a waiting period between shots. Find out all possible side effects.

➤ Even though we live in a time of increasingly imper-
sonal medical care, try to befriend a nurse in your
doctor's office so you have a trustworthy, caring coun-
selor if you have serious concerns while traveling. Be
sure to carry your physician's phone number when
you travel.

➤ Pack liquid antihistamine for young children (in your
carry-on bag for airplane travel) and capsules for
yourself and your older children. If someone has a
cold, it will help clear sinuses to reduce pressure and
pain on airplane landing. An antihistamine can be
helpful to control rashes and itching if someone has
an allergic reactions to eating shellfish, too much
sugar, or strong chlorine in pools.

➤ If your child is susceptible to motion sickness, pack a
large, strong, locking plastic bag and always carry
medication such as Dramamine.

➤ When traveling with
small children who are
prone to ear infections,
ask for a prescription
from the pediatrician
which does not require
refrigeration. For a nat-
ural alternative, a warm
dropper full of garlic/
mullien oil to both ears
is soothing and has
antibiotic properties.

➤ If you are crossing time
zones, allow time to
recover from jet lag. Go

> _____ \\\\|//_ _____
>
> *I travel everywhere with a*
> *homeopathic health care book*
> *and travel kit with 20 or so*
> *remedies. With these I can take*
> *care of many kinds of emergen-*
> *cies—food poisoning, motion*
> *sickness, burns, bites, sprains,*
> *fevers, and more. They are*
> *safe, non-toxic, and can be*
> *used by all ages from infant*
> *through adult.*
>
> ◆
>
> Wenda Brewster, Ph.D., 49,
> writer

easy the first few days. It is also good to spend time outdoors at your destination to reset your circadian clock. Do your best right away to adapt to the time zone, even if it means keeping the kids up when they want to sleep because at home it is midnight. Otherwise you will be playing cards with them in the middle of night as their body adjusts to the new time.

> *I always take packets of "Emergen-C," a vitamin C powder from which you can make a refreshing drink, and multivitamins my children call "disgusto pills" for their powerful smell. Their real name is Wellness Formula, and they are the single best thing I take when travel wears me down.*
>
> ◆
>
> *Jasmine Harris, 33, waitress*

➤ Be extremely cautious with drinking water in developing countries. Freezing water to make ice cubes doesn't kill the germs. Order drinks without ice. Check the seal on bottled water.

➤ If you are going to a place where travelers' diarrhea is common, consider carrying electrolyte supplements. If your children get severe diarrhea, they should increase fluid consumption, eat bland dry foods, and rest while you seek medical assistance.

➤ If you absolutely cannot wash your hands, rubbing your hands rapidly together can kill many germs through friction.

➤ If you or a member of your family has persistent diarrhea upon return from vacation, ask your doctor to run tests to eliminate the possibility that you are carrying a parasite.

➤ If you travel in a country where malaria is a concern (Africa, South America, Asia), ask what malarial medicine works in that region. Also ask tropical disease specialists what effect that particular medicine has on young children—some are too harsh for kids to take.

Instant Hand Sanitizer is a great new product that kills germs without having to use any water.

◆

Kathy Measure, 48, airline account executive

➤ In developing countries, think twice about allowing children to eat ice cream or other dairy products, including custards, cream fillings, and mayonnaise. You can't be sure if the milk has been pasteurized or the product has been properly refrigerated.

➤ Seafood can carry hepatitis, so be careful about where and what you eat. If you are not certain that it is fresh and clean, eat it only if it has been thoroughly cooked. Especially avoid raw seafood, which can carry cholera, if you have any doubts.

➤ Carry lots of sunblock. Apply first thing in the morning whether you are in the snow, at the beach, or touring a city.

➤ Always travel with a first aid kit that includes: a needle, tweezers, bandaids, bandages, tape, antiseptic cream, basic liquid motrin, antihistamine, icepack, and a bottle of ipecac onto which you have written the 800 number for the national poison center.

➤ Prepare your children for bathroom facilities in other countries, whether it be the use of a bidet or a pit

toilet, as well as the varying types of toilet paper
substitutes.

➤ Carry a mini-medical summary that includes list of
shots, allergies, medical conditions, medications, and
blood type of each family member.

➤ If you or your children wear glasses or contact lenses,
bring spares, including a spare bottle of saline solution.

➤ If something serious occurs overseas, seek out the
hospitals that serve the international community in
major cities. Call your embassy for a reference.

➤ Consider carrying your own needles, along with a
note from a physician, for extended off-the-beaten
path trips.

XI

MOTHERS IN SPIRIT

One can never pay in gratitude; one can only pay "in kind"
somewhere else in life.

—*Anne Morrow Lindbergh,* North to the Orient

━━━━━━

MANY WOMEN do not have children of their own, yet they mother children all over the world. My friend Olga Murray, a retired 71-year-old San Francisco attorney, spends half of every year with her children in Nepal. There are 275 of them now, many of them blind or deaf, many with cerebral palsy or other disabilities. They have lived in the streets of Kathmandu on the fringes of their own society and as outcasts from their families. The street children of Kathmandu are Olga's life now. She set out on her first trek in 1984 and went to see the Himalayas, but it was the children that kept her coming back.

Travelers can change the world. Rather than a wild adventure, traveling can be intensely civilizing and humanizing. Recently, as Olga was packing her bags for Nepal, she told me, "Person-to-person, soul-to-soul, a traveler begins to understand the world and her place in it—as a human being with value and purpose, among other human beings with value and purpose."

Personally, I have been deeply touched by the people I've met while traveling. I have found there are many ways to give something back, either on the spot or upon return. It is possible to make a big difference in someone's life at a modest cost. Years ago, on a trip to Nepal, our trekking group created a "Sherpa Scholarship Fund" and made donations for the next three years, to enable our guide,

Ringee, to attend university-level studies. He later told me that upon landing his first job he sent his first paycheck home to his father, a widower, so he could use it for a good dowry for his sister.

Judy, another friend, has opened her life to a motherless teenager through the Little Sister Program. She shares her world with this one special girl. Over the years they have experienced farm life, city life, outdoor adventures and family holidays together. You don't have to travel far to nurture. Women like Olga and Judy are changing the world, one woman at a time. (See the "Resources and References" chapter for further details on opportunities to get involved.)

We have thousands of lepers. They are wonderful, they are admirable, even though their flesh is disfigured. Every year we offer the lepers a Christmas party. Last Christmas I told them that they have a gift from God, that God has a special love for them, that they are very acceptable to God, that what they have is not a sin. An old man who was completely disfigured, tried to get close to me. He said, "Say it again. That has been good for me. I have always heard that no one loves us. It is wonderful to know that God does love us. Say it again."

◆

Mother Teresa, Missionary of Charity and Nobel Laureate

TIPS

➢ After you arrive in a country look up the foreign groups that have an office in the main city, such as Save the Children or World Vision. They can refer you to other foreign aid organizations that might need volunteer help for a week or two. Opportunities somehow present themselves if you take the initiative.

➢ When traveling off-the-beaten track into areas where

you are likely to make personal contact with other mothers, take some children's clothing and make a gift of it to someone who shows a kindness or with whom you have spent time. It is always warmly welcomed and appreciated. On the flip side, the emotional reward you will get by giving things away is much greater than the few dollars you might realize by selling them at a garage sale.

➤ Consider volunteering at an orphanage. They are often shorthanded and the presence of a stranger to play with the children is very welcome.

➤ Teaching English is a great way to volunteer and it is not necessary to have formal teaching credentials to do so. In developing countries where English can be the road to success, many schools welcome a friendly

_____ ⸕⸕⸜⸝ _____

On my first trip to Tijuana, I saw a woman on the street, begging. She had a toddler and an infant to take care of at the same time as she begged. My house-building teammates and I pooled our spending money. We took her to the grocery store and bought food and diapers for her and her children. She cried tears of gratitude. I cried for the joy of helping someone who had less than I had. It really is "more blessed to give than to receive!"

◆

Tim Williams, 15, high school student

_____ ⸕⸕⸜⸝ _____

When I was an exchange student living in a home in Tokyo many years ago, I learned you don't have to have biological ties to someone to nurture them like your own child. My Japanese mother took me in like the daughter she never had.

◆

Judy Jacobs, 45, writer

foreigner who will give English conversation classes.

➤ Do you play a musical instrument? Consider bringing it with you, or taking up the harmonica or penny whistle. Music and song are invaluable communication tools, and will help you bridge many language and cultural chasms.

➤ In developing countries only the wealthy own cameras. One of the nicest things you can do is send photographs to people whose pictures you have taken during your travels. Many of us collect names and promise to do this but don't follow through. The time and expense involved really are minimal, though, when you consider that what you send may be the only photos these folks have of themselves or their children.

➤ If you're traveling with children and your kids meet other kids along the way, set up a pen pal arrangement. If the family can't afford stamps, you can go to the post office and make a gift of enough stationery and stamps to ensure the project gets off the ground.

➤ You don't have to travel far to nurture others. International Student Exchange Programs, The Girl

_____ ⚡ _____

My children have traveled mostly in Europe, with a few excursions into Mexico and the Caribbean, so they haven't been exposed to a great deal of raw poverty, but nonetheless their travels have made them think a lot more about less fortunate kids. Each of my daughters now sponsors a child through World Vision, and they try hard to earn extra money around the house so they can send small gifts and make a monthly contribution to their little charge abroad.

◆

Jasmine Harris, 33, waitress

Scouts of America, Big Sister Programs, Homeless
Shelters, Shelters for Abused Women and School
Tutoring Programs in communities near you are beg-
ging for volunteers.

➤ Consider a volunteer vacation or begin your stay in
each new country with a homestay. These are excellent
ways to get beneath the surface of a culture and find
ways to make a difference. (See "References and
Resources.")

_____ \\\\\|/// _____

*For the past five years I have been sponsoring a child through Children
International. Most people have seen the ads on TV, and most people react
skeptically. I myself wondered if my money was directly benefiting the child
or if it was underwriting a huge administrative operation. By wonderful
coincidence, this child lives in Ecuador and I had a business conference in
Quito. The organization's staff in Kansas City were delighted to arrange a
meeting which I would have never thought possible. Not only was I able to
meet my sponsored child, but her mother as well. Both knew exactly who I
was—my family's photo, sent three years ago, was displayed in their home.
I was given a tour of the Children International project in her village on the
outskirts of Quito, an area without water, plumbing, paved roads, or schools.*

◆

Ruth Limtiaco, 40+, founder, president, public relations firm

XII

ℳOTHERING IN 𝒪THER ℭULTURES

...travel is more than the seeing of sights, it is a change that goes on, deep and permanent, in the ideas of living.

—Miriam Beard, American writer

———————

MOTHERS IN TRADITIONAL CULTURES worldwide have much to teach us about being a mother in our own culture. I have been fortunate enough to live in homes with indigenous mothers in many diverse cultures, seeing them go about their daily lives, teaching, guiding and loving their children. I have brought home many valuable lessons about successful mothering.

In a Sherpa home in the Annapurna range of the Himalayas a beautiful young mother juggled many roles: cook, house cleaner, water carrier, fuel collector, provisioner and hostess of guests who slept on the floor next to the family and her newborn baby. Despite the heavy burden of three children under the age of three, Dawa never showed any signs of stress or impatience with her guests or family. She seemed at ease and content in her well-defined roles. She enjoyed the respect of her husband and fellow villagers for her skill to raise children

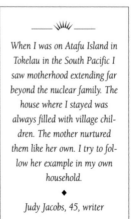

When I was on Atafu Island in Tokelau in the South Pacific I saw motherhood extending far beyond the nuclear family. The house where I stayed was always filled with village children. The mother nurtured them like her own. I try to follow her example in my own household.

♦

Judy Jacobs, 45, writer

and simultaneously run a lucrative business in her home. She never complained or hesitated to devote her loving attention to a needy child or trekker. She is not alone in her love of mothering. While living in other homes, I have witnessed this same joy, grace, resilience, and patience among mothers in many cultures, from the Hmong in northwestern Vietnam to the Irish dairy farmer on the Dingle Peninsula.

A Nepali friend once told me that her entire family gets together and plays instruments and sings. She said that in Nepal this is perfectly natural. Every child learns how to sing. She explained that is their way of celebrating life.

Can we incorporate into our lives what we learn from mothers in other cultures? Yes, some aspects are easy. Women around the world keep their babies swaddled and in constant contact with their bodies. Even when they are in the fields,

Over several decades of photographing in remote areas, I evolved a method of quickly integrating when I went into villages with complete cultural and language barriers. I was such an oddity for them as a woman photographer. I would give my camera to children and let them look through it. Everyone —moms, grandfolks, and kids—would burst into giggles. They would crawl all over me and handle all my gear. Although my initial reaction was to be protective of my equipment and space, I learned they needed to touch everything. It was part of their culture. I developed the mother's instinct to broaden my boundaries and understand that the most important thing is to share joy, be generous, and communicate happiness and feeling. It is more important than being possessive of your own goal. Abandon your ego objectivity and it will all work for you. It has been a critical lesson as a photographer, a human being, and now as a mother.

♦

Pam Robertson, 49, professional photographer

kitchens or markets, they carry their babies on them. From the example of mothers in traditional cultures I learned the importance of touch.

There are basic, instinctual ways to be a mother. Mothers in traditional cultures seem closer to nature, the earth, and to their basic instincts. We must get back

> *I remember the Argentinean mother of a teenage exchange student who lived in our home. She called me repeatedly, asking me to remind her son to study his biology. We had a lot in common. Moms share the same concerns everywhere.*
>
> ◆
>
> *Shelby Brough, 51, traveler*

in touch with our instincts and not doubt our innate sense of how to nurture and love. We too must believe in ourselves and learn from the continuity of generations, wisdom passed down from grandmother to mother and mother to child.

TIPS

➤ Host a student from your intended destination prior to your trip, to observe their habits and better understand and appreciate their culture.

➤ When you arrive in a foreign place, ask locals how outsiders should greet and treat children. For example, in Thailand, one shouldn't pat children on the head as the head is considered the abode of the soul.

➤ Arrange a stay with a family. Staying with mothers in traditional cultures I've observed that it is possible to remain calm and patient even under the most trying circumstances. Mothers are the heart of the family, and maternal strength, patience, and stability set the tone for everyone. Mothers who put their children and families before their own wishes most of the time appear to have less inner conflict.

➤ If you are invited to participate in family life in indigenous cultures, jump in, don't hold back. You can't help but notice the importance of singing and dancing. In some cultures the poetry and songs a mother shares with her children have been passed down for gener-ations. Ask about the meaning and origins of songs and dances, and consider the importance of reciting poetry or verse and singing songs to your children which are part of your family history or heritage.

> _A Balinese child is never allowed to touch the ground for the first year. They are always in someone's arms. I've watched Thai and Indonesian mothers who have continual physical contact with their infants. When we adopted our son he was 4 years old. I had almost constant physical contact with him for the first few months to speed up our bonding._
>
> ◆
>
> Marilyn Staff, 40+,
> tour company founder

➤ Observe the behavior of mothers in traditional cul-tures—you can learn a lot. I saw through their exam-ples that you can never touch your children too much. When they are young, hold them on your lap, caress their tiny legs and arms, carry them on your hip, chest or back. If they are accustomed to your touch, then even when they are older you can start every day with a hug and use touch (hugs, pats, back rubs and neck rubs) as a way to comfort them.

➤ Take note of children developing self-esteem and responsibility by handling important family chores. We must make our children responsible for part of the family life—making their beds daily, helping to make dinner, doing the dishes, setting the table, cutting the grass—and increasingly take on more responsibility as they grow older. There is no free ride for children in other cultures and our own children must learn this lesson, too.

➤ Be mindful that mothers in traditional cultures remain close to the earth and share this wisdom with their children. If we expose our children to the beauty, bounty, and blessings of nature, they learn to appreciate and draw upon its soothing and rejuvenating strength.

> _Living among the Luo tribes in Kenya for two years I was amazed at the amount of responsibility mothers give to their young children. Chores that were vital to the family's well-being, such as gathering wood, collecting water, tending infant siblings, and herding cows. They often had no choice but the result is self-sufficient youngsters. My challenge as a parent is to find meaningful responsibilities for my children that contribute to our family as well._
>
> ◆
>
> _Liz Cornish, 43,_
> _former medical director_

XIII

𝒫REGNANT 𝓜AMAS 𝓗IT THE 𝓡OAD

Oh what a power is motherhood,
Possessing a potent spell.

—*Euripides*

PREGNANCY DEFINITELY REQUIRES adjustments to a daily routine but it need not tie you down. Unless you are one of the few women who experience continuous morning sickness for nine months, your life should continue to be exciting with a little more time scheduled for naps!

During pregnancy we are usually more conscious of diet and exercise, and generally need more rest and plenty of fluids. This may take a bit of extra planning if you are traveling outside the U.S. Remember, pregnancy is not a sickness. It is completely natural and women have been having babies and traveling for millennia.

I traveled from the jungles of Costa Rica to the chateaux of the Loire during my first pregnancy. During my second pregnancy I didn't travel overseas at all, for many reasons: I had a young infant, I had become more cautious, and I had learned that there is a fine line between being gutsy and being foolish. Travel during pregnancy to developed

In Asian countries such as India and Pakistan where pregnancy is a celebrated and private occasion, pregnant woman usually stay close to home. If you look very pregnant, you might feel uncomfortable in public and may attract stares.

◆

Mary Bakht, 42,
public relations

countries is quite safe if a woman is healthy, and I was. However, the exhaustion and potentially poor diet caused by travel during pregnancy is not healthy. When traveling I often wished I could lie down for an afternoon nap, or walk into my own kitchen to blend a protein-filled fruit smoothie to satisfy my constant hunger.

There are special considerations for pregnant women traveling whether in the first, second, or third trimester. Everyone should be cautious if traveling in the last months when alternative delivery plans may be necessary. If you are traveling to remote areas or places far from conventional maternity care, extra caution should be taken.

Prior to my trip to Costa Rica I consulted with my obstetrician and learned of potential problems that I had not considered. A recent outbreak of measles among women in their 30s in the U.S.A. raised questions about the duration of vaccinations given to school age children two decades ago. Consequently, today women are encouraged to be revaccinated prior to conceiving. Not only had I not been revaccinated, but I also discovered that I had never had a rubella vaccination. Most children in the U.S. have been vaccinated and are not carriers. However, the story is

> ⎯⎯ 〜〜 ⎯⎯
>
> *I discourage pregnant women from traveling to underdeveloped countries because of the potential risk to mother and child. Find out if you can be air ambulanced out, or you may return with a big scar up and down your belly, and your uterus removed. In many developing countries the blood supply is tainted with HIV, Africa most notably. Delivering a baby can be a very bloody business. You may need ten units of blood for a hemorrhage. Catastrophes do happen. Better to have them happen here than abroad.*
>
> ◆
>
> *Kimberly Mulvihill, M.D., 41, obstetrician/gynecologist*

quite different in developing countries. My obstetrician warned me to stay away from schools, school-age children, and anyone sick, because they are the most likely to carry these diseases. During the entire trip I shuddered every time someone coughed or sneezed near me. Advised not to take anti-malarial medicine, I was obsessed with preventing insect bites. I didn't want to run the risk of catching malaria so I smothered my body in bug repellent, sprayed my hair, clothing, and hotel rooms

Take a serious look at all the vaccinations you will need. Ask yourself, "What if I have a miscarriage?" and tailor your plans accordingly. A pregnant patient of mine had a D & C overseas and it was complicated by an infection. She is now unable to conceive and the rest of her married life she and her partner will have to deal with her infertility. They may be able to say "What a great trip we had" but there can be other, very serious consequences.

♦

Deborah Rosinski, M.D., 54, obstetrician/gynecologist

and I didn't get a single bite! (Of course, be aware that bug repellent containing a lot of DEET might be harmful to your unborn child.)

Unlike Costa Rica, I was sure that traveling to Paris and the Loire Valley in the springtime would be safe and simple. I looked forward to indulging in French pastries, cheeses, and patés. I had given up caffeine as soon as I learned I was pregnant and I adhered strictly to the dietary recommendations of guidebooks and my doctor. I soon learned that I needed to pack, plan, and eat differently than I had on previous trips. I couldn't enjoy the typical French breakfast of strong coffee, butter croissants, and bread. I craved protein. While my friends were leisurely sipping their final café-au-laits in the hotel, I scurried down to the corner café, bellied up to the bar, and ordered a large orange juice, two hard boiled eggs and a baguette for my second breakfast. I carried herb tea in my purse to drink when I normally would have indulged in espressos. All in all I had a marvelous trip with only minor adjustments to my schedule, diet and packing.

Deliver overseas? If you are part of the U.S. military, rest assured that their hospitals offer excellent care and the physicians are trained in the USA. The major cities in developed countries also have hospitals and health care equal to that available in the USA. If you plan to travel in the developing world during your third trimester be sure to research your options for childbirth.

To travel or not to trav-el, how much and where, when you are pregnant is a question all mothers must ask themselves. Before you make the decision to travel overseas, ask yourself, "What diseases are endemic in this area? What season am I going to be traveling in this area? Monsoon? Cold and flu season? What vaccinations will I need? What medication should I take with me? What medications will I be required to continue taking upon my return, for how long, and with what consequences?" If you are going to err, err on the conservative side.

> ───── ⋰⋰⋰ ─────
>
> *I traveled to Finland and Russia when I was three months pregnant. The cigarette smoke on the plane made me extremely nauseous. I carried a towel in my backpack every-where in case I got morning sickness and needed to throw up. I flew over the Pole and went in a sauna in Finland. Only later did I learn that I'd taken a risk. Some studies say flying over polar regions expos-es you to increased radiation and most American doctors advise against saunas and hot tubs for fear of raising your internal temperature and dam-aging the fetus. These experi-ences caused me to worry a lot during the pregnancy.*
>
> ◆
>
> Janet Fullwood, 44,
> travel editor

TIPS

➤ Make a mental note to use the ladies' room prior to a flight, car, or train trip. Pregnancy increases pressure on the bladder. Women are also more likely to get bladder infections during pregnancy so it is very important to empty your bladder on a regular basis.

➤ When traveling by plane or train, get up every two hours, walk around for five minutes, and stretch to enhance circulation and prevent swelling in your legs. Blood circulation in the pelvic area is reduced when sitting for long periods.

➤ Carry a big bottle of water on board airplanes and drink no caffeinated drinks during your flights.

➤ When flying, avoid small unpressurized planes where the supply of oxygen to the fetus can be diminished. Try to book a seat in the front of the plane or over the wings where you will feel less motion and as far from possible from the galley where the smell of food may make you nauseous.

➤ Eat lightly when you fly, drive, or travel long distances because during pregnancy you are more prone to motion sickness.

_____ \\\\|//_ _____

My husband and I honey-mooned in Kenya and the Seychelles Islands in the Indian Ocean. With the possibility of conceiving a baby, I did not want to take the usual malaria prophylactic, which can induce birth defects for up to six months. I contacted the CDC and was able to take a common broad-range antibiotic for the same anti-malarial effects. This turned out to be a very good thing; nine months later, we had a beautiful baby boy.

♦

Brenda Davis, 37, full-time mother of four

➤ It is easy to miss meal times when traveling, so carry nutritious foods such as hard-boiled eggs, raw fruit and vegetables, seeds, nuts, dried fruit and crackers to fill in when you don't have balanced meals. Pack hard candy in your purse to help prevent nausea caused by low blood sugar.

➤ Pack your prenatal vitamins and mineral supplements. If in doubt about the cleanliness of tap water, take your pills with and drink only bottled water.

> *Pregnancy is a very short period in a woman's life and she should do everything possible to ensure the health of the developing fetus so we recommend that she reserve travel to risky areas for another time in her life. The vaccinations required for travel to most developing countries have not been adequately tested for safety during pregnancy. Even a trip to Mexico can be hazardous if a woman gets a case of turista and becomes dehydrated. You certainly don't want to go to a hospital in a foreign land where you don't speak the language.*
>
> ◆
>
> *Linda Goldberg, 58, obstetrical nurse practitioner*

➤ After 30 weeks of pregnancy, if you are very big, carry a note from your obstetrician stating exactly how pregnant you are. Airlines have been known to deny boarding to very pregnant-looking women.

➤ Anyone who considers traveling beyond 37 weeks should check with their insurance carrier. Many big health care plans say you're grounded in terms of delivery coverage past 37 weeks. Often they will not cover you if you travel over 50 miles away. Delivering when you're uninsured could cost $5,000 or more. If you have to travel to a funeral or for a personal emergency, obtain a written approval from your insurance company prior to traveling.

➢ Scuba diving is off limits, but snorkeling is fine, according to obstetricians.

➢ In France and many parts of Europe, consuming unpasteurized cheeses or milk products can lead to an infection of listeria. Listeria can lead to a serious intrauterine infection in the mother that can be passed to the baby and cause premature birth.

➢ To avoid salmonella, eat only well-cooked chicken, pork and beef. Eat no raw eggs for the same reason (you'll have to pass on the Caesar salad).

➢ Be sure to get enough calcium so your calves do not cramp and cause you undue distress.

➢ When traveling domestically, ask your obste-

_____ ⚜ _____

We spent over two months in Europe on our honeymoon and have fond memories early in the trip of Belgian chocolate, Irish salmon, French wine, and Norwegian goat-cheese. But then something happened. The food didn't taste so good anymore. Our travels were curtailed by my sudden inability to get on a bus. Those vistas we would scramble up a mountainside to get, well, now they just made me plain old nauseous. Yep, I was pregnant. The worst of it was in Rome. Through a friend, we were put up in a room on an empty floor of a hospital run by Little Sisters of the Poor. We had lots of privacy, including our own hospital beds. My husband had even more privacy, as he toured the sights alone! It was appropriate that we were in a hospital, as I needed to lay in bed most of the day. And it was so convenient to have a pregnancy test done "in house." We celebrated when a little white envelope was slipped under our door, with the result, "positivo."

♦

Angelique Syversen, 36, mother of seven

trician or midwife to give you a name, address, and phone number of a physician to contact where you are traveling, if you should need help.

➤ Prior to foreign travel, consult with your obstetrician as well as a specialized overseas medical clinic, such as the Centers for Disease Control, about the vaccinations you will need and which ones should be avoided when pregnant. The official statement from the CDC, says that all live viral vaccines, such as typhoid, measles, mumps and rubella, are not recommended during pregnancy.

> *Giving birth in a developing country is a gamble. If you have a normal pregnancy and everything goes well during the delivery, you'll probably have no problems, but if you have a problem you may not find the quality of care available to you in the US and you won't have reliable backup. Once it is done you can't go back and change it, you and your child will have to live with the consequences for a lifetime.*
>
> Charlie Evans, 42, Emergency Medicine M.D., former physician in Africa bush hospital

➤ If you are trying to conceive, take note: if you take malaria medication, you must continue taking it for an extended period of time after your trip, (up to 6 months). It is recommended that you wait 3-4 months after you go off this medication before you try to conceive.

➤ Not pregnant yet, but thinking of trying during a long trip? Many obstetricians recommend you stay on birth control pills when traveling. Your risk of having significant problems will be decreased, such as developing a cyst on an ovary or having a heavy period the first month you go off the pill.

➤ During travel, wear comfortable, loose fitting clothing. Depending on the stage of your pregnancy, you may want to wear a back support or tummy cradle.

_____ ⚘ _____

When I was seven months pregnant with our second child, we left our two-year-old daughter at home with a close friend and went to Mexico. My husband and I snorkeled, hiked in the desert, and swam in the ocean. My great moment of glory was winning a sailboat regatta with another very pregnant woman as crew.

◆

Wenda Brewster, Ph.D., 49, writer

XIV

$\mathcal{T}$RAVELING $\mathcal{A}$BROAD FOR $\mathcal{A}$DOPTION

Love seeks not limits but outlets.

—*Anonymous*

———

MANY PARENTS ARE CHOOSING ADOPTION as a way of creating their families, and international adoption is a choice which requires a great deal of research, education, commitment, and above all, patience. Access to the World Wide Web and online chat rooms can help you figure out the details of the travel and the red tape in your chosen country of adoption. You cannot be too prepared for this adventure, whether you choose an agency, a facilitator, or go off on your own. Read everything you can get your hands on and pose your questions to experts more than once, and from as many angles and contingencies as you can think of.

People have quite different experiences, even in the same country of adoption. Who you meet and what is going on politically in the country of adoption will lend itself to a unique experience. I was told time and again by adoptive mothers that this trip will be unlike any others you have ever taken or will ever take again. You will travel in a way you don't normally travel and have experiences you would rarely have as a tourist—going into police stations, embassies, and people's homes (you may spend a lot of time in your lawyer's home, for example.)

When you travel to the country of adoption, expect to have a powerful life experience. Relax and be open to the fact that many things will happen you may not have planned on. Picking up your child in a foreign country, you will have the greatest opportunity to absorb input—verbal, emotional, and cultural—if you hold yourself open to this unique experience. Returning to their country of birth years later will not be the same. Now is the time to pay attention and learn as much as you can. It will give flavor to your stories later in life when you communicate with your child about their country of birth. Adoptive mothers told me repeatedly that this journey is like giving birth. And like birth, no amount of preparation can really prepare you for the reality.

> *I was encouraged to dress casually, and I think it's good advice. Not a lot of jewelry and fancy, expensive-looking clothes. You might not be aware of all cultural mores, so dressing simply is an easy way to make sure you're not drawing attention to yourself and your child. Westerners have a more open attitude toward adoption than many other countries, some of whom question our motivations.*
>
> ◆
>
> Janet Boyd, 36, graphic artist

TIPS

➤ Even if you've never kept a journal before, keep one during your travels to adopt. You're going to be a new parent with all the time constraints that implies, but try to get even just one meaningful sentence a day on paper. It will serve you and your children well by triggering lots of day-to-day memories that would otherwise get lost.

➤ When planning your adoption budget, figure in a lump sum for international phone calls. If only one of a couple is traveling, or if you have other children waiting at home, you're going to want to talk frequently. If you're traveling alone, that home connection could be very important. It also pays to look into which is less expensive: having someone call you from home or having you make the call.

➢ Another unexpected expense can be for gifts and bribes. This doesn't apply to all countries, but you may be expected to bring small gifts for several of the people who were going to be helping you in the country of adoption, such as the orphanage staff, even though you may never meet them. Check with your agency early on in the process to see if issues like this will apply to your situation.

➢ Have your pediatrician give you a prescription for a general antibiotic. You can travel with it in powdered form, so it doesn't need refrigeration, and reconstitute it if and when needed. Review with your doctor other medications it may be good to have along, both for your child and for you.

➢ If you know you'll be away for quite some time and left pretty much to your own devices, it wouldn't hurt to bring some easy-to-prepare dried foods. Boxed meals, a jar of peanut butter or dried soup mixes will sustain you for days at a time when you don't have the wherewithal to actually cook anything.

➢ Learn some simple phrases in your child's native language. If adopting an older child, it will give some instant access to communicate directly with them. It is also a sign of respect to those who were helping you and stumbling along in English.

➢ Don't expect to bond with your child immediately. For

some people that happens, but the majority of the time, there's so much going on for all of you, that it won't. Whether your child was well cared for or not before coming to you, they will have a grieving process to move through while adjusting to their new

When I adopted in Romania, I was expected to bring twenty cartons of cigarettes and many pounds of coffee for gifts to people I never met. The gifts and bribes really added up and cut into my traveling money.

♦

Sue Willing, 41,
print coordinator

life. The sensory input can be overwhelming. Some children shut down and sleep heavily for days. Others are physically ill and need to heal. Still others seem to bounce off the wall with joy.

➢ You may find that your child will go to anyone as willingly as they go to you. Please don't take that personally. They're still figuring out that you're the special one(s). Just try to follow their lead.

➢ While still in your child's country of origin, ask as many questions as you can about your child's history, his/her likes and dislikes, food preferences, pet peeves. Delve into the culture, the language, the history. It's the best opportunity you'll have and you don't know when you might get back there. You can then hold this information in trust for your children if and when they have questions.

➢ For some families, your stay abroad may be a lengthy one while you wait for paperwork to go through. Taking a few short local trips to get a feel for where you are is a nice thing to do, but you really need to follow your child's lead. Some children may have never been outside the orphanage, so walking down a busy street, in a stroller, seeing sights and smelling smells may be all they can handle.

➤ Keep all the scraps of paper and other tidbits that make up your trip. Plane tickets, visa notices, some currency from your child's country of origin, etc. will all be great things to put in a scrapbook for them.

➤ Make a decision before you leave if you want a welcoming committee to greet you at the airport when you arrive home. Some people prefer to just have their immediate family there and go home for a few days of privacy. For others, it's great fun to have as many friends as possible there to meet you. However you do it, arrange to have someone there with a camera and/or video. The airport visit should be short and sweet and the party should NOT move to your house. You're going to have jet lag and your child is going to be dizzy from so much activity. Head home and spend the rest of your lives sharing your child with your loved ones.

➤ If you feel any reservations about cultural differences between you and the child you are adopting, spend some time absorbing the culture of his or her birth country.

> ───── ☀ ─────
> *Bring good walking shoes! If at all possible, try to learn the language basics of the adoption country. We adopted a beautiful 18-month-old girl from Mexico. We were detained for seven weeks in a hotel room waiting through "unexpected" delays. Bring lots of reading material.*
>
> ◆
>
> *Marti Harrison, 48, high school teacher*

- ➢ If you are in the process of adopting an older child and find that friends are scheduled to travel to the adoptive country, have them bring your child gifts and photos of yourself. They can also take pictures of your child for you.

- ➢ Make double and triple copies of all your documents. Keep each set in separate places.

- ➢ Budget between $15,000 and $35,000 per person traveling to countries of adoption. This includes airfare, taxis, car rentals, food, hotel rooms, gifts, emergency child care items, and tips (bribes).

- ➢ If you need a translator, try to arrange it from the USA. Translators can be expensive. Inquire at local universities; this may result in substantial savings down the road.

- ➢ Many companies grant maternity leave during your adoption process.

- ➢ If at all possible, travel with a friend or spouse. You will need the moral support and extra help when you are bringing your child home.

_____ ⚡ _____

I learned that even if your child appears quite relaxed, they're under a great deal of emotional stress as well as being exposed to new environments. For instance, my daughter had NEVER been outside the orphanage she lived in her entire lifetime when I adopted her. The one day trip I took with her into the mountains of Romania was a great break for me but a mistake for her. She cried the whole time and didn't take one bottle all day.

♦

*Sue Willing, 41,
print coordinator*

➢ Take pictures in your child's country of origin: the orphanage, the first contact, and so forth. Also purchase culturally relevant toys and pictures to bring home.

"How much did he cost?" That was one of the most frequent questions our local Cantonese friends asked us after we adopted our 14-month-old Hong Kong Chinese boy—a typically frank query for money-minded Cantonese. "Isn't he dark!" they grimaced, when summer days spent on Hong Kong beaches turned him a nut brown (gorgeous to us but not to those who consider pale skin an indication of high class). Now that we've adopted a second Chinese child, we're into a whole new vocabulary of compliments (or otherwise): Lia's huge eyes are "ho leng" (very beautiful), her chubby size a definite thumbs-up (Cantonese love food as much as money; the fatter you are, the more you can afford to eat). And look at that head of hair! (Another indication of wealth to come, lucky us). In fact, she doesn't look Chinese at all—she must be from the Philippines, yes? (not a compliment, for the Cantonese tend to look down on local Filipinas). But they seem to love the children nonetheless and, in Cantonese eyes, we've been raised to sainthood for "taking the risk" of adopting them.

◆

Julia Wilkinson, 41, author and journalist

XV

$\mathscr{P}$LANES, $\mathscr{T}$RAINS AND $\mathscr{A}$UTOMOBILES

She looked out the window…savoring the extreme pleasure of
being on a moving train with nothing to do for six hours but
read and nap and go into the dining-car.

—*Stanley Edgar Hyman,* The Magic of Shirley Jackson

THE KEY TO GETTING THERE, whether you go by plane,
train, or automobile, is preparation. Not only do you need
the reservations, tickets, and maps, you'll also need things
to keep you and your children happy—toys, games, books,
snacks, and ear plugs. They need to be involved in preparations for the travel part of your vacation too. If they pack
their own carry-on bag, they can choose their own entertainment and snacks. Boredom and hunger can make any
kid cranky.

Long car trips can be
tough on children because
they are so confined. If your
road trip starts early in the
morning you may be able to
carry little ones snuggled up
in their favorite blankets
into the pre-packed car and
hope they will fall back to
sleep. If your children are
older, consider an active
hike, swim, or frisbee game

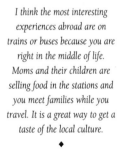

*I think the most interesting
experiences abroad are on
trains or buses because you are
right in the middle of life.
Moms and their children are
selling food in the stations and
you meet families while you
travel. It is a great way to get a
taste of the local culture.*

◆

Judy Jacobs, 45, writer

before departure, so they have already worked off some
energy.

Train travel is exciting for kids as long as it is not for too long. It is more adventurous than driving in the family car, they can move around and explore the dining car, snack bar, lounge car, and restrooms. Kids often meet other kids on the train, switch seats, and play with new companions. Some trains feature sightseeing lounge cars with picture windows from floor to ceiling. Several trains offer special family fares and kid-friendly meals in the dining cars. If you are planning a cross-continental trip with your family, consider calling Amtrak for information on their rates and services. Then you can compare costs for train travel vs. a car trip.

> *We put a cardboard box between the kids in the car to separate them. In the box we keep sketch books, colored pencils (each has a set so they won't fight over them), magnetic car bingo , a cassette or CD player, headphones, tapes or CD's for each child, and large-size card games. I add something new (and keep it a surprise) for each trip. The "car box" never comes into the house. It definitely works for us.*
>
> ◆
>
> *Joy Norris, 39,*
> *marathon athlete*

When you are traveling by plane you'll have a different set of pleasures and challenges with children. Whenever you fly, give yourself plenty of extra time at the airport.

Whether you travel by road, rail, boat, or plane, the following tips may make your journey a little smoother.

TIPS

➤ When traveling with an infant or small child in an airplane, it is important to help them clear their ears upon take-off and landing. This can be achieved by breast-feeding, giving a bottle, or using an eyedropper. With the eyedropper, just fill with any liquid and periodically put drops in their mouth to make them swallow. Constant swallowing helps clear their ears and makes for a happier baby.

➤ Try to get seat reservations at the bulkhead when traveling with an infant or small child in an airplane. Not only is there additional floor space to change diapers, but many airlines have a portable crib-like device which screws into the bulkhead. Small infants can sleep comfortably in it, but the crib cannot accommodate children that are older than 4 or 5 months.

➤ Kids usually don't like airplane food. Call at least 24 hours prior to departure to order a special kids meal or pack fruit, sandwiches, bags of "goldfish," or other treats.

➤ Each child should carry aboard the plane, train or car a reading book that they intend to read. Also suggest they bring along a diary and drawing notebook.

➤ Allow time for things to go wrong. A twenty minute connection with kids in tow is asking for chaos.

➤ When you travel, consider having "no-sugar days." The kids are calmer and less fussy, whether it is a plane, train, or automobile, and when you get to your destination everyone can have a special treat for being a good traveler.

➤ When flying, take along earplugs for the whole family as well as eye masks. Especially good are the eye masks which allow you to open your eyes while you are wearing them—which can be easier on children.

➤ If you have the time, look into train travel before you hop in the car or book an airline ticket. Amtrak and the trans-Canadian trains offer comfortable sleepers, dining cars and views from dome ceilings. The price for train travel is comparable or slightly higher than the cheapest air fares, but you will see so much more of America. You will discover our trains are filled with young European students traveling on youth fares from coast to coast and north to south. Check it out.

> _Before a long plane trip I buy my children brand new reading materials, dot-to-dot books, the latest Nintendo game, and other fun arts and crafts items. To make it special I wrap them up as if they were a birthday present, with ribbons and the works. When they put on their seat belts I bring out the presents. They love it and it keeps them busy._
>
> ◆
>
> Julia Zalles, 40+, counselor, fabric artist

➤ If you are a family of five or more, remember that you may not always be able to travel in the same taxi. Plan accordingly.

➤ If you are renting a car, ask the agency what type of child seat fits in their rental vehicles.

➤ On car trips, travel with picnic fixings (sandwich makings, fruit, drinks, blanket, thermos). Having a picnic in a park or even at highway rest area lets everyone stretch legs as well as fill their stomachs quickly.

➤ If you rent a car, stop at a grocery store nearby and buy a twelve pack of soda or juices. You'll prevent a lot of whining and save money. Drinks on the road can be few and far between and expensive.

➤ If your child gets car sick, kitty litter is good for absorbing odors and moisture.

➤ Take a break from dri-
ving every couple
hours. Use rest stops on
highways to let kids run
around and let off
steam. Keep an activity
bag in the car with
balls, frisbee and other
sports items for use on
these breaks.

➤ A round-robin game that is suitable for both adults
and children of school age to play in most modes of
transportation is a naming game based on the alpha-
bet. Someone begins with a word based on a theme
(states, famous people, animals), the next person has
to come up with another word based on the last letter
of the first word (i.e., California → Arizona →
Alaska, etc.) . You can vary the game by looking out
the window and using passing scenery as the theme.

XVI

$\mathcal{P}$LANNING, $\mathcal{P}$ACKING, AND $\mathcal{B}$UDGETING

A vacation frequently means that the family goes away for a rest, accompanied by a mother who sees that they all get it.

—*Marcelene Cox, American writer*

WE KNOW WHO USUALLY does the vacation planning in most families and who is responsible for keeping costs in check: mom. I recommend you start planning early, be resourceful, and don't give up if you are unsuccessful at first in locating the perfect vacation destination or an airfare you can afford.

One year I waited until May to begin organizing our family trip to major national parks in July. We decided to rent a recreational vehicle (RV) so we could enjoy "sissy" camping. We wanted the nightly campfires, bears lumbering through our campsites, and the family-friendly ambiance of campgrounds along with the privacy and comforts of home that an RV provides. I began calling for reservations and discovered that all the national RV companies had rented all their vehicles months earlier. So then I called local Chambers of Commerce in three cities

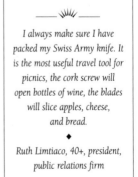

I always make sure I have packed my Swiss Army knife. It is the most useful travel tool for picnics, the cork screw will open bottles of wine, the blades will slice apples, cheese, and bread.

♦

Ruth Limtiaco, 40+, president, public relations firm

where we could begin our trip to the national parks. An employee in each office was kind enough to look through the yellow pages and give me the phone numbers of local RV rental companies. Twice we rented vehicles directly from the owners, who charged less than the big companies and they even picked us up at the airport. It pays to be creative and to keep trying.

Staying within your vacation budget is a major concern for all moms. Budget killers include: eating all meals out, especially breakfast, eating in restaurants without kids menus, waiting until you get to the "resort" to do your grocery shopping, forgetting everyone's raingear, warm jackets, or swimsuits.

Before I leave I photocopy all my travel documents (passports, drivers licenses, credit cards) and pack it in a separate bag from my purse. I include on this page: telephone numbers for contacting credit card companies (in case of theft), our doctor's phone numbers in case I need advice, and all our blood types.

♦

MBB

Budget savers include: staying in hotels with buffet breakfasts included in the price, traveling off-season when airfares are less and hotels are half-empty, staying outside of a city as opposed to downtown near the tourist attractions, locating home exchanges or home rental agencies.

Become a Sherlock Holmes when planning your travels. Make it a game and bring other family members into the hunt. Get kids to go to the library for books and delve into the Internet. Just search under the name of the place you are going and you will be surprised what comes up on the screen. Even the town of Angels Camp in the California Gold Country has a web page, along with many Chambers of Commerce, bed & breakfasts, and national parks in the United States. Their pages usually list accommodations, activities in the area, and special deals. You can print out the information you like and staple it together for your own guidebook.

And never forget that you won't get a discount if you don't ask for it.

TIPS

Packing and Planning

➤ Making key lists and using them when preparing for a vacation helps you minimize shopping trips for supplies. The greatest benefit of using lists to pack is that you will forget fewer essential items, like fresh batteries for flashlights or dental floss.

➤ Pack plenty of ziplock bags of all sizes. They help organize dirty clothes or keep wet bathing suits separate from dry items.

➤ Make phone calls to park rangers, hotels, and tourist offices and ask them for advice on where to stay, what to see and about economical ways to visit. It never hurts to ask: "Is there a cheaper way to go?"

➤ Use your AAA membership. Order maps and the accommodation, restaurant and camping guidebooks as soon as you choose your destination. They list all price ranges. If you go to an AAA office they

When our family flies to Hawaii we always take a box of food. The box can be checked through just like luggage and saves us quite a bit of money in food costs. We take dry goods such as cereal, pasta, snacks, syrup, muffin mix, and other staples.

◆

Susan Brady, 38, production coordinator

have a tour desk with people who will help you map your route and make reservations.

➤ When packing travel clothes rely on a layering system, especially if traveling to a cold climate. Start with lightweight long underwear made of a fast-drying material than add layers. Pack one layer of fleece clothing (pants, tunic, jackets). Fleece clothing packs compactly, is light-weight, easy-care, and dries quickly so you can wear it every day and wash it every evening.

➤ Kids do best with comfortable mix and match clothes for traveling. Every child needs two bathing suits, a hat, windbreaker, sneakers, sandals, and a large cotton t-shirt that can double as a nightgown or bathing suit cover-up.

➤ Although my children are not afraid of the dark, in a strange place or setting they like to sleep with a night-light on. Always pack one, along with a flashlight for trips to the bathroom.

➤ Pack a small sewing kit with scissors.

➤ Leave space in your bags so you can bring home souvenir t-shirts, sweatshirts, or other thick items. That way you won't be forced to buy an additional bag enroute. Some travelers always bring an extra rolled up lightweight nylon duffel with them for goodies bought along the way.

➤ Bring breakfast food or buy it as soon as you get to a destination—cereal, juice boxes, etc. You'll save a bundle. If you stay in one place try to get a room with a refrigerator or a minibar.

➤ Involve your children in the planning from the very beginning. Then the older ones have a stake in the success of the trip and the younger ones know what to expect. After you have poured over all the brochures and material you can collect, have everyone make a list of what they want to see and do.

> ─── ⸜⸌ ───
>
> *On flights on wide-bodied planes, I usually reserve the aisle seat in the middle section with an empty seat or two between my son and me. When I arrive at the airport, I can usually find out from the ticket counter agent which seats aren't taken yet. This way we can stretch out or play games on the seat between us.*
>
> ♦
>
> *Phyllis McCreery, 33, yoga teacher*

➤ Carry copies of birth certificates and passports when traveling in foreign lands.

➤ Carry phone numbers of all credit card companies so you can cancel immediately if they get stolen and so that a new one can be issued.

➤ Teach your children to be good packers. Help them develop a packing list and collect a pile of things to take days ahead of time. Then make a game of their reducing what they've packed by 20%. Help them think through what they'll be wearing and using during the trip.

Budgeting

➤ If possible, travel off season. There are few lines and economy rates.

➤ Budget motels can save you a lot of money. They may

not offer all the amenities, like a concierge, coffee shop on-site, wall-to-wall carpet or a health spa. They usually provide the basics—clean rooms, air-conditioning, television and occasionally a swimming pool or jacuzzi. Some of these chains provide a roll-away bed

> _Involve teens in the planning and preparation of the trip. We like to have a voice regarding our vacation, then we know what to expect, and will be eager to help make the vacation more memorable._
>
> ◆
>
> Angela Torzala, 15,
> home school student

or crib at no extra charge and allow kids under eighteen to stay free in their parents' room. Always ask.

➢ Ask hotels and car rental agencies what clubs, credit cards, or other membership associations they honor for discounts.

➢ Look for accommodations that include a free breakfast.

➢ Try taking a vacation with another family to cut costs. Consult with other family members about who to invite. Plan your trip with the other family. Two heads are better than one and you'll have less gear to pack if you share items.

➢ Consider renting a condo, cabin, or beach house with a kitchen and prepare all your meals there.

➢ Call a city's Chamber of Commerce prior to your departure and ask which museums, events, or parks are free. Sometimes they are staffed by older "mom" volunteers who will offer you some valuable insiders information. The Chamber can give the museums' phone numbers to inquire about docent tours and programs for children.

➤ The more you research a destination or vacation, the more money you will save. Travel agents can't spend hours on each client. They are likely to book you into a resort, or large chain hotel. You'll need to do research yourself to find information on discount accommodations. Call hotel booking services (listed in the "Resources and References" Chapter) or the local Chamber of Commerce and ask about B & B's and budget hotels. Check out the yellow pages of your destination city at the library or do research on the Internet.

XVII

$\mathcal{V}$ACATION $\mathcal{I}$DEAS

What I hear, I forget.
What I see, I remember.
What I do, I know.
—*Chinese Proverb*

———

RIGHT AFTER THE WINTER holidays, my husband and I begin to fret over our travel plans for summer. How shall we spend our precious vacation? What is our budget? How far do we want to go? How can we please everyone? What can the kids reasonably tolerate? What would the kids most enjoy? What is our passion? What do we really want to do and where do we really want to go? Choosing the destination, activities and possible travel companions for your vacation is both challenging and time-consuming.

In our busy lives, the path of least resistance is often following the advice of a friend or work associate. You hear someone rave about a resort, dude ranch, family camp, bike trip, or beach house and you follow their example without giving serious consideration to your own dreams. Sometimes this works out well, and sometimes it doesn't. It is not easy to decide upon a destination or activity for a vacation.

Those of us who traveled with our families when we were young usually want to revisit our favorite places with our children. I want to relive many special memories, such as seeing my first shooting star on a camping trip in the Rockies, rafting down the Snake River at dawn—bull moose grazing along the shore—or driving across the planes of Wyoming amid herds of wild antelope and not seeing another vehicle for hours.

Most of us want to travel farther than we did as children. I would like to explore Bali, Nepal, France, Spain, Thailand, and other far-flung destinations with my family. But then, I am a dreamer and my wanderlust is insatiable. I do try to keep my children's ages and abilities in mind as well as my husband's desires and our budget! So every vacation is a compromise. And yet, as the years pass, our summer family trips get better and better because we put more time and thought into selection and planning. We are beginning to understand what works and doesn't work for us.

When children are young, it is best to start out with simple excursions, such as short trips to a local hotel, beach, lake or mountain resort, or a weekend camping trip close to home. As your children get older and you are more experienced traveling with them, advance to more exotic locales and more physical activities.

In this chapter you'll find ideas for vacation destinations and activities. Use your imagination and expand on the basics provided to plan a great vacation. The last chapter, "Resources and References," provides specific names and phone numbers to help you begin your planning. Bon Voyage. I hope to meet you on the road, trail, train, plane, boat, raft, or safari vehicle!

ACTIVITIES AND DESTINATIONS

➤ Road Trips with an RV (ages 0+). Renting a recreational vehicle to cruise and camp through the national parks is a great vacation for families of all ages. It is particularly easy when you have infants and toddlers, as they can nap and be fed easily while traveling. And you only have to unpack once! Campgrounds are great places for children to explore creeks and forests and to meet other kids. Consider renting in Phoenix, to visit the Grand Canyon and Indian territory, or start in Salt Lake City for a trip to the Grand Tetons and

Yellowstone, or fly north to Calgary, Canada to tour the uncrowded and spectacular Canadian Rockies.

➤ Club Med Family Vacations (ages 0+). Club Med provides children with time together as well as time apart in the guaranteed company of other kids. They offer free stays for teens in some destinations depending upon the month of travel. Activities include sailing, windsurfing, kayaking, snorkeling, swimming, circus training, mountain biking, golf, horseback riding, squash and archery. Kids learn new skills and meet others their own age from all over the world, while parents relax or partake in a wide variety of sports and activities.

➤ Resorts (ages 0+). Most resorts and large hotels offer both child care and day camps. Some of the kid's programs are just glorified baby-sitting services, so ask lots of questions. Two outstanding exceptions are Club Med and the resorts in Hawaii. In Hawaii the youth programs emphasize Hawaiian history, culture, and geography with diverse activities—nature walks, sand-volcano building, tide-pool exploration, petroglyph walks, native arts and crafts, and storytelling.

➤ Water Vacations (ages 2+). Let's face it, kids love to play in water! Whether you rent a beach house or a cottage on a lake or river, what they may well remember best is playing at the water's edge. As long as there is water, preferably a beach with sand, tide pools, or shells, kids will entertain themselves for hours. Consider kayaking as a family in ocean waters or wilderness lakes and rivers. There are two and three-person kayaks so a parent can take a young or inexperienced child on calm water.

➤ Camping (ages 2+). Starting to camp early in life pre-
pares your children for any kind of travel. They learn
to love being in the outdoors and can entertain themselves making imaginary horses out of stumps with
grass manes and string bridles, or catching insects.

➤ Theme Parks (ages 4+). You have a wide choice all
across the country, from Disneyworld in Florida to
Disneyland in California, with numerous Sea Worlds,
water parks, and amusement parks in-between. I prefer parks that combine amusement, education, and
entertainment, like Sea World, Disneyworld, or historic
Williamsburg.

To help you make the most of your visit to a theme
park, to maximize your good memories and minimize
your frustration and fatigue:

• If you can, avoid visits on weekends or school
holidays.

• Arrive before the opening time and hurry to the most
popular ride first. Do your homework so you know
what and where it is.

• Make a priority list of rides, shows, and activities
that includes something for each child.

• If possible, have one adult wait in line while the
other takes kids to the bathroom, scopes out other
rides, or buys food.

• Be realistic about how much a young child can
appreciate, enjoy, or remember.

➤ Family Camps (ages 4-17). Family camps can be ideal
family vacations. Many are learning centers with class
schedules that might include: beginning rock climb-

ing, ropes course 101, elementary sailing or whitewater kayaking, and mountain-biking. You will watch your children acquire new skills, new friends, and self-confidence. Numerous alumni groups, the YMCA, Outward Bound, and the National Wildlife Federation offer summer family camps in spectacular mountain or lake setting. Accommodations are usually in wooden cabins or bunkrooms. There are organized activities for all ages groups. Mom can relinquish her roles of cook, maid and chief organizer for the week. Some are an economical way to enjoy the outdoors, relax, and meet other families. For most of the university camps, you do not have to be an alumni to participate. (See "Resources and References" chapter).

➤ Dude ranch vacations (ages 5+). Dude ranches offer unlimited possibilities for the rider to explore picturesque backcountry, for the angler to catch a trout, for the trekker to hike forest trails, and for tired parents to kick back in a rocking chair and bask in the tranquility of secluded mountains. Supervised youth programs are offered by staff and ranches foster a warm family atmosphere. Your children will be exposed to wilderness, new friends, hayrides, campfire sing-alongs, action and relaxation, cowboys, horses, and honest hospitality.

➤ Family cruises (ages 5+). Major cruise lines are welcoming families with children to cruise aboard their fleets of luxury liners in popular destinations like the Caribbean and Alaska and are offering special children's fares. Triple and quad staterooms make it easy and comfortable to bring the kids along or plan a family reunion that includes all generations. Several cruise lines offer on-board activity programs for kids 5-17.

Ask if the cruise line offers shore excursions for youth, kids menus at dinner, and the chef's specials for children.

➤ Eco-Travel and Nature Trips (ages 8+). Taking your family into the wild gives them an opportunity to explore nature and learn about the environment in a hands-on way. In the United States, plan trips to where the wild things are: grizzlies in Denali National Park in Alaska, whales in the Sea of Cortez, sea otters off the coast of California near Monterey, or moose in Grand Teton National Park, Wyoming.

➤ River rafting adventures (ages 9+). These are a great vacation for parents and kids. Families with younger children can stick to float trips in moderate white water, Class I to II rapids, where experience and special skills are not required. Families with teens may opt for rivers with more intense whitewater for bigger thrills. Or you may choose an experience that combines both, such as the Colorado River through the Grand Canyon.

➤ Bike trips (ages 10+). If you have the time and equipment, you can plan a do-it-yourself bike trip—simply map out routes, prepare your meals and accommodations, then toss the bikes on the trunk rack of the car and go. There are also bike tours and bike camps that include guided rides, beginner routes, instruction, bike and gear rentals, and lodging.

➤ International trips, fully outfitted and guided, can be expensive, but I highly recommend spending your money on a once-in-a-lifetime family odyssey—a trip your kids will still be talking about in 2040! An African safari, an ecotrip to the Galapagos Islands to

swim with seals and see birds with blue feet, to
Australia to ride camels, feed kangaroos, and snorkel
the Great Barrier Reef, or a heritage tour to the land of
your ancestors.

XVIII

_D_R. _C_ULBERTSON'S
_A_ TO _Z_ _E_XCURSIONS

Whether you are in your backyard or the farthest-flung corner
of earth, all the mysteries and wonders of life are right there
in front of you.

—*Anonymous*

FOLLOWING IS a generic list of places to visit whether
you're traveling close to home or far away. It is not a com-
prehensive list, but a point of departure. It was compiled
and contributed by Diana Culbertson, Ph.D., 61, a retired
teacher and librarian who has taken children to many of
these locales. Add to the list and make it a game with your
children—see how many kinds of places you can visit in a
year, make a list of all the things you've already seen, done,
learned, and talk about the memories that gush forth.

Antique shop, Archery Range, Aquarium, Arboretum,
Airport, Art Festival, Amusement Park, Auction,
Automobile Factory, Archeological Dig

Battlefield, Book Store, Bus Ride (local, long distance),
Bus Station, Boat Ride, Band Practice, Balloon Flight
(ride/look), Basketball Game (Professional, non-profes-
sional) , Baseball Game, Bird Watching, Blacksmith, Boat
Show, Bowling, Botanical Garden, Bakery, Beach

Church, Concert, Clock Shop, Craft Store, Camping,
Cheese Factory, Candy Factory, Coin Show, Carousel Ride,
Craft Show, Cemetery, Coffin Maker

Displays of all types (check local paper and libraries), Dance Studio, Dance Recital, Diamond Hunting in Arkansas

Egg Hatchery, Excavation Sight

Fire Station, Flag Shop, Florist, Farms, Fairs, Football Game, Factories, Fish Hatchery

Go Kart Race, Gym, Gem Show, Graveyard, Garbage Dump, Gold-Panning

Hang Gliding, Horse Race, Horse Fair, Harness Race, Hot Air Balloon Ride, Hospital

Ice Hockey Game, Indian Display (check stores, libraries)

Jump Rope Competition (Heart Association sponsors these in most schools each year), Jewelry Maker

Karate Demonstration, Kite Flying, Kangaroo Watching

Library, Lighthouse, Lapidary Store, Lake

Museum, Mountain Climbing, Mineral Store, Movie, Music Store, Mines (various types), Moon Watch (astronomy clubs sponsor these on a regular basis), Mall, Marathon

Neighborhood Centers, Nurseries, Natural History Museum, Native American Village

Organizations (check phone book), Organ Recital, Olive Grove, Organic Farm, Orchard

Post Office, Parks (local, state, national, historical), Puppet Theater, Parade, Planetarium, Pet Shop, Pow-wow

Quarry (rock, salt), Quilt Demonstration

Recreation Center, Race Track, Railroad Station, Railroad Display, Rock Climbing, Recycling Center

Ski Life, Swap Meet, Sports Show, Soap Box Derby, Subway, Synagogue, Science Center, Sewage Treatment Plant

Train Station, TV Studio, Theater, Tennis Match, Thrift Shop, Taxidermist

Uranium Exhibit, Upholstery Exhibit

Volleyball Game

Weather Station, Water Purification Plant, Wallpaper Store

Xmas Pageants, Programs and Displays, xylophone factory, "X marks the spot"—geographic centers of states and regions, e.g. the center of France, the center of Washington State

Yacht Club, Yard Sale, Youth Center

Zoo, zoological research station, zebra photography

XIX

$\mathscr{R}$ESOURCES AND $\mathscr{R}$EFERENCES

A travel adventure has no substitute. It is the ultimate
experience, your one big opportunity for flair.

—*Rosalind Massow, American writer*

———

Family Programs, Resorts and Tour Operators

Colorado Trails Ranch
12161 County Road 240, Durango, CO 81301-6306
800-323-3833

Club Med Resorts
40 West 57th Street, New York, NY 10019
800-CLUB MED

Overseas Adventure Travel (minimum age: 10)
625 Mt. Auburn Street, Cambridge, MA 02138
800-221-0814

Rascals in Paradise (no minimum age)
650 Fifth Street, Suite 505, San Francisco, CA 94107
800-872-7225

Intergenerational Travel

Elderhostel
75 Federal St., Boston, MA 02110
617-426-8056

Grandtravel/Ticket Counter, Inc.
6900 Wisconsin Ave. Suite 706, Chevy Chase, MD 20815
800-247-7651

SPECIALIZED TRAVEL SERVICES
FOR FAMILY ADVENTURES

Archaeology Trips and Dinosaur Digs

Denver Museum of Natural History (minimum age: 5)
2001 Colorado Blvd., Denver, CO 80205
303-370-6304

Dinosaur Discovery Expeditions (minimum age: 6)
550 Crossroads Court, Fruita, CO 81521
800-344-3466

Earthwatch (minimum age: 10)
Box 403, Watertown, MA 03372
800-776-0188

Bike Trips

Appalachian Valley Bicycle Touring
P.O. Box 27079, Baltimore MD 21230
410-837-8068

Backroads (minimum age: 6)
1516 5th St., Berkeley, CA 94710
800-462-2848

Vermont Bicycle Touring (minimum age: 10)
Box 711, Bristol, VT 05443
800-245-3868

Covered Wagon Trains

Myers Ranch Wagon Trains (minimum age: 6)
Box 70, Ismay, Montana 59336
406-772-5675

Oregon Trail Wagon Trains (minimum age: 5)
Route 2, Box 502, Bayard, NE 69334
308-586-1850

Teton Country Wagon Trains (minimum age: 4)
Box 2140, Jackson, WY 83001
800-772-5386

Athabasca Cultural Journeys (minimum age: 8)
Box 10, Huslia, AK 99746
800-423-0094

Four Corners School of Education
P.O. Box 1029, Monticello, Utah 84535
800-525-4456
fsc@igc.apc.org

Best Cruise Lines for Families with Children

American Hawaii Cruises
800-765-7000

Carnival Cruise Lines
800-327-9501

Disney Cruises
800-551-8444

Holland America CruiseLine
800-426-0327

Royal Caribbean Cruise Lines
800-327-6700

Dude Ranches

There are too many to list individually. I suggest you start
by writing or calling some of the following organizations:

American Wilderness Experience (no minimum age)
Clearinghouse representing ranchers, outfitters, and dude ranches
Box 1486, Boulder, CO 80306
800-444-0099

Dude Ranch Association
Represents over 100 ranches
Box 471, LaPorte, CO 80535
970-223-8440

Colorado Ranchs
12161 County Road 240, Durango, CO 81301-6306
800-323-3833

Family Camps

Tuolumne Family Camp
Outside Yosemite National Park
510-644-6520

National Wildlife Federation
800-754-2913

Outward Bound School
Family Alpine Adventure
800-477-2627

Hiking and Backpacking Trips

Appalachian Mountain Club
Box 298, Gorham, NH 03581
603-466-2727

Camp Denali (minimum: 6)
Box 67, Denali National Park, AK 99755
907-683-2290

Canadian Mountain Holidays (all ages)
Box 1660, Banff, Alberta, Canada
800-661-0252

Sierra Club (all ages)
730 Polk St., San Francisco, CA 94109
415-923-5522

Horse and Llama Pack Trips

Avalon Llama Treks (minimum age: 4)
450 Old Buckeye Cokve Road, Swannanoa, NC 28778
704-299-7155

Derringer Outfitters (minimum age: 10)
Box 157, Quemado, New Mexico 87829
505-773-4860

Hurricane Creek Llama Treks (minimum age: 6)
63366 Pine Tree Road, Enterprise, OR 97828
505-432-4455

Northern Vermont Llama Company (all ages)
R.R. 1 Box 544, Waterville, VT 95492
802-644-2257

River Rafting

American River Touring Association (minimum age: 6)
Representing trips on five rivers in the Western USA
24000 Costa Loma Road, Groveland, CA 95321
800-323-2782

AZRA Arizona Rafting Adventures
Grand Canyon raft trips
4050 E. Huntington Dr., Flagstaff, AZ 86004
800-786-7238/520-526-8200

Sheri Griffith Expeditions (minimum age: 5)
Box 1324, Moab, Ut 84532
800-332-2439

Idaho Afloat (minimum age: 6)
Box 542, Grangeville, ID 83530
800-700-2414

O.A.R.S. Rafting Adventures
Box 67, Angels Camp, CA 95222
209-736-4677

Rivers & Oceans Travel
P.O. Box 40321, Flagstaff, AZ 86004
800-473-4576

Overseas Family Adventures

Overseas Adventure Travel (minimum age: 10)
625 Mt. Auburn Street, Cambridge, MA 02138
800-221-0814

Sea Trek Ocean Kayaking Center
P.O. Box 561, Woodacre, CA 94973
415-488-1000

Baja Discovery (minimum age: 5)
Box 15257, San Diego, CA 92195
800-829-2252

Asia Trans Pacific Adventures
P.O. Box 1279, Boulder, CO 80306
800-642-2742

Working Cattle Ranches and Cattle Drives

Montana High Country (minimum age: 12)
669 Flynn Lane, Townsend, Montana 59644
406-266-3534

Adventure Travel Advisory Service
7550 E. McDonald Dr., Scottsdale, AZ 85250
602-596-0226

Organizations Specializing in Women's Travel

Wild Women Adventures
Women-only guilt-free getaways worldwide
107 N. Main Street, Sebastopol, CA 95472
800-992-1322

Rainbow Adventures
Worldwide adventure travel for women over 30
15033 Kelly Canyon Road, Bozeman, MT 59715
800-804-8686

Womentours
Bicycle Tours for Women
PO Box 931, Driggs, Idaho 83422
800-247-1444

Great Old Broads for Wilderness
Women only trips to protect wilderness, hike, have fun
1942 Broadway, Suite 206, Boulder, Colorado 80302
303-443-7024

Roots & Wings Excursions
Travel Adventures for Mothers & Daughters
423 Carlisle Drive, Suite A, Herndon, VA 20170
800-722-9005/303-443-7024

RVing Women
P.O. Box 1940, Apache Junction, AZ 85217.
1-888-55-RVING (888-557-8464)

Volunteer Opportunities and Mother in Spirit Organizations

Big Brother/Big Sister
1-800-288-4543

Earthwatch
P.O. Box 403, Watertown MA 02272
617-926-8200

Global Exchange
2017 Mission Street # 303, San Francisco, CA 94110
415-255-7296

Global Volunteer
Short term opportunities for all ages
375 East Little Canada Road, St. Paul, MN 55117
800-487-1074

Habitat for Humanity
Volunteers help build homes in more than 32 countries
322 West Lamar Street, Americus, GA 31709
800-422-4828

Nepal Youth Opportunity Foundation
for Kathmandu Children
203 Valley Street, Sausalito, CA 94965
415-332-4589

Operation Crossroads Africa
150 Fifth Avenue, New York, NY 10011
212-242-8550

RSVP
Retired and senior volunteer programs in 36 countries
500 5th Avenue, 35th floor, New York, N.Y. 10110
212-575-1800

SERRV International
Works with small cooperatives and nonprofits in developing countries to ensure a fair price is paid to artisans
800-423-0071
www.serrv.org

TERN (Traveler's Earth Repair Network)
Friends of the Trees Society
P.O. Box 164, Tonasket, WA 98855

Worldteach
Volunteers with bachelor degrees teach English for one
year in developing countries
Harvard Institute for International Development
1 Elliot Street, Cambridge, MA 02138-5705
617-495-5527

World Vision
To sponsor a poor child in another country
P.O. Box 78481, Tacoma, WA 98481-8481
800-777-5777

Youth Service International
301 North Blount Street, Raleigh, NC 27601
800-833-5796

SAVING ON YOUR VACATIONS

AAA Travel Services 800-272-2155
Mention AAA membership when booking any travel. As a
member you can obtain AAA Travel Insider, catalogue of
members-only cruise and tour discounts, AAA Tour
Books, Bed & Breakfast Guide, maps, and more.

AARP American Association of Retired Persons
Available to anyone over age 50
Discounts and special rates available for members.
800-424-3410

Hotel Consolidators

Hotel Reservations Network
800-96-HOTELS

Quickbook
800-789-9887

House Swaps and Homesays

Friendship Force
Suite 575, South Tower
One CNN Center, Atlanta, GA 30303
404-522-9490

House Exchange Program
952 Virginia Ave., Lancaster, PA 17603
717-393-8985

Interhome
124 Little Falls Road, Fairfield, NJ 07004
201-882-6864

International Homestays
Foreign Language/Study Abroad Programs
Box 903, South Miami, FL 33143
305-662-1090

Intervac/International Home Exchange
Box 59054, San Francisco, CA 94519
415-435-3497

LEX Homestay in Japan
LEX America
68 Leonard Street, Belmont, MA 02178
617-489-5800

Servas
11 John Street, New York, NY 10038
212-267-0252

Vacation ExchangeClub
Box 820, Hale'iwa, HI 96712
800-638-3841

Villas & Apartments Abroad, Ltd.
420 Madison Avenue, New York, N.Y. 10017
212-759-1025

REFERENCE, READING, AND RESEARCH

CDC (Centers for Disease Control)
Atlanta, GA
404-332-4559
404-332-4565 (to request information to be sent via fax)

Homeopathic Educational Services
Mail order house with catalog of homeopathic
books, remedies, travel and home kits
2124 Kittredge St., Berkeley, CA 94704

Peters Projection World Map
Friendship Press
P.O. Box 37844, Cincinnati, OH 45222

*Adventuring with Children: The Complete Manual for Family
Adventure Travel*
Nan and Kevin Jeffrey
Avalon House Publishing, 1991

Dinosaur Safari Guide
Lists over 150 museums, parks, quarries, and trails
Vincenzo Costa
Minnesota: Voyageur Press

Everybody's Guide to Homeopathic Medicines
Stephen Cummings, M.D. and Dana Ullman, M.P.H.
New York: Jeremy P. Tarcher/Putnum Books, 1991

Family Travel
Evelyn Kaye
Colorado: Blue Penguin Publications, 1993

Fodor's Family Adventures
Christine Loomis
New York: Fodor's Travel Publications, 1996

Homeopathic Medicine at Home
Maesimund B. Panos, M.D. and Jane Heimlich
New York: J.P. Tarcher

Innocents Abroad: Traveling with Kids in Europe
Valerie Wolf Deutsch and Laura Sutherland
New York: Penguin Books USA, 1991

The International Adoption Handbook: How to Make Foreign Adoption Work for You
Myra Alperson
New York: Henry Holt and Company Inc.

The Peace Corps and More: 120 Ways to Work, Study and Travel in the Third World
Meda Benjamin and Andrea Freedman
Carson, California: Seven Locks Press, Inc. 1989

The Pocket Doctor: Your Ticket to Good Health While Traveling
Stephen Berushka, M.D.
Seattle: The Mountaineers, 1988

Take Your Kids to Europe
Cynthia W. Harriman
Mason-Grant Publications, 1991

Trading Places: The Wonderful World of Vacation and Home Exchanging
Bill and Mary Barbour
Tennessee: Rutledge Hill Press, 1991

Traveling with Children and Enjoying It: A Complete Guide to Family Travel by Car, Plane, and Train
Arlene Kay Butler
Connecticutt: Globe Pequot Press, 1991

Travels with Children - a travel survival kit
Maureen Wheeler
Hawthorne, Australia: Lonely Planet Publications, 1990

Trouble Free Travel with Children: Helpful Hints for Parents on the Go
Vicki Lansky
Minnesota: The Book Peddlers, 1985

The Vacation Home and Hospitality Exchange Guide
John Kimbrough
Kimco Communicatons, 1991

Volunteer Vacations: A Directory of Short Term Adventures That Will Benefit You and Others
Bill McMillon
Chicago: Chicago Review Press, 1995

WORLD WIDE WEB RESOURCES

There is a lot of information about women's organizations on the Web, and to learn how to find it go to the **Traveler's Tales Web Site** (www.ora.com/ttales), scroll down to the link for Web Tours, and pull up the Women's Travel Page. Here is a sampling of what you'll find:

Accomodations
Women's Hospitality Exchange International Network
Internet Guide to Hosteling
Hostels Europe
Hostelling International
Landfair Home Exchange

Guidebooks and Planning:
Other *Travelers' Tales* books
Your Trip Abroad

Sites for Women on the Net:
Blue Stocking
Cybergirl
Fabulous New Women
FeMiNa
Girls Internationally Writing Letters (Penpals)
Pleiades Network: An Internet Resource for Women
Virtual Sisterhood
Women's Wire

Also search under Languages, Health, Currency, Transportation, Statistics, Demographics, and Security.

$\mathscr{I}$NDEX OF
$\mathscr{C}$ONTRIBUTORS

―――

$\mathscr{A}$ BOUT THE $\mathscr{A}$ UTHOR

MARYBETH BOND lived in Paris for four years, Luxembourg and New Caledonia for one year. At the age of 30, fed up with a corporate job in the computer industry, she took off to travel solo for two years around the world. She has trekked across the Himalayas, the Andes, and the Alps, ridden camels across the Thar and Sahara Deserts, and elephants through the jungles of Asia. Today, she has two jobs, two kids, two mortgages, a husband, and a dog. She lives in Northern California and writes, consults for Overseas Adventure Travel, and gives keynote speeches.

Marybeth's first book, *Travelers' Tales: A Woman's World*, is an eloquent collection of women's writing that paints a rich portrait of what it means to be a woman today. *A Woman's World* won the Lowell Thomas Gold Medal for Best Travel Book from the Society of American Travel Writers Foundation. She has appeared on CNN, CNBC, America Online, and National Public Radio to share travel tips and discuss how women travel differently than men.

Whenever she can she travels—with her children, husband, girlfriends, her mother, or alone.

TRAVELERS' TALES GUIDES

LOOK FOR THESE TITLES IN THE SERIES

TRAVELERS' TALES
GUTSY WOMEN
TRAVEL TIPS AND WISDOM FOR THE ROAD

By Marybeth Bond
ISBN 1-885211-15-5, 124 pages, $7.95

Packed with instructive and inspiring travel vignettes, *Gutsy Women: Travel Tips and Wisdom for the Road* is a must-have for novice as well as experienced travelers.

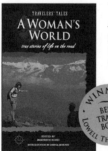

TRAVELERS' TALES
A WOMAN'S WORLD

Edited by Marybeth Bond
ISBN 1-885211-06-6
475 pages, $17.95

"I loved this book! From the very first story, I had the feeling that I'd been waiting to read these women's tales for years. I also had the sense that I'd met these women before. I hadn't, of course, but as a woman and a traveler I felt an instant connection with them. What a rare pleasure."

—Kimberly Brown, *Travel & Leisure*

TRAVELERS' TALES
A DOG'S WORLD

Edited by Christine Hunsicker
ISBN 1-885211-23-6, 232 pages, $12.95

"The stories are extraordinary, original, often surprising
and sometimes haunting. A very good book."
—Elizabeth Marshall Thomas, author of
The Hidden Life of Dogs

TRAVELERS' TALES
THE ROAD WITHIN

Edited by Sean O'Reilly,
James O'Reilly & Tim O'Reilly
ISBN 1-885211-19-8, 443 pages, $17.95

"A revolutionary new style of travel guidebook."
—*New York Times News Service*

TRAVELERS' TALES NEPAL

Edited by Rajendra S. Khadka
ISBN 1-885211-14-7, 423 pages, $17.95

"Always refreshingly honest, here is a collection that
explains why Western travelers fall in love with Nepal
and return again and again."
—Barbara Crossette, *New York Times* correspondent and
author of *So Close to Heaven: The Vanishing Buddhist
Kingdoms of the Himalayas*

TRAVELERS' TALES FOOD

Edited by Richard Sterling
ISBN 1-885211-09-0, 444 pages, $17.95

"Sterling's themes are nothing less than human
universality, passion and necessity, all told in stories
straight from the gut."
—Maxine Hong Kingston, author of
The Woman Warrior and *China Men*

TRAVELERS' TALES BRAZIL

Edited by Annette Haddad & Scott Doggett
ISBN 1-885211-11-2, 433 pages, $17.95

"Only the lowest wattage dimbulb would visit Brazil
without reading this book."
—Tim Cahill, author of *Jaguars Ripped My Flesh* and
Pecked to Death by Ducks

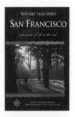

TRAVELERS' TALES SAN FRANCISCO
Edited by James O'Reilly,
Larry Habegger & Sean O'Reilly
ISBN 1-885211-08-2, 432 pages, $17.95

"As glimpsed here through the eyes of beatniks, hippies, surfers, 'lavender cowboys' and talented writers from all walks, San Francisco comes to vivid, complex life."
—*Publishers Weekly*

TRAVELERS' TALES HONG KONG
Edited by James O'Reilly,
Larry Habegger & Sean O'Reilly
ISBN 1-885211-03-1, 438 pages, $17.95

"*Travelers' Tales Hong Kong* will order and delight the senses, and heighten the sensibilities, whether you are an armchair traveler or an old China hand."
—Gladys Montgomery Jones
Profiles Magazine, Continental Airlines

TRAVELERS' TALES PARIS
Edited by James O'Reilly,
Larry Habegger & Sean O'Reilly
ISBN 1-885211-10-4, 424 pages, $17.95

"If Paris is the main dish, here is a rich and fascinating assortment of hors d'oeuvres. *Bon appetit et bon voyage!*"
—Peter Mayle

TRAVELERS' TALES SPAIN
Edited by Lucy McCauley
ISBN 1-885211-07-4, 452 pages, $17.95

"A superb, eclectic collection that reeks wonderfully of gazpacho and paella, and resonates with sounds of heel-clicking and flamenco singing—and makes you feel that you are actually in that amazing state of mind called Iberia."
—Barnaby Conrad, author of *Matador* and *Name Dropping*

TRAVELERS' TALES THAILAND
Edited by James O'Reilly & Larry Habegger
ISBN 1-885211-05-8, 405 pages, $17.95

"This is the best background reading I've ever seen on Thailand!"
—Carl Parkes, author of *Thailand Handbook*,
Southeast Asia Handbook by Moon Publications